Jesse James, My Father: The First and Only True Story of His Adventures Ever Written

BY

Jesse James Jr.

Leo

CHAPTER I.THINGS I REMEMBER OF MY FATHER

I was born August 31, 1875, in Nashville, Tenn. I recall with vivid distinctness an incident that occurred in Nashville, when I was about five years old. At that time my father, Jesse James, was away from home. Dick Liddill was staying at our home during the absence of father. It was the night of St. Valentine's day. While mother and myself and sister and Dick Liddill were at home, there was a sound as if someone was throwing rocks against the front door. Dick started to open the door, but mother suspected that it was someone who had discovered who we were and were trying to entice Dick out to capture or kill him. She would not allow him to open the door. Dick then got my father's shot gun from a closet. Both of its barrels were loaded heavily with buckshot. Before my mother could interfere to prevent it, Dick aimed at the door and fired the charge of buckshot, tearing a great hole through the door panel and splintering it. Dick rushed to the door and threw it open and ran out on the porch. In the darkness he saw a man running around the corner. Dick fired the second barrel straight at him, barely missing him, the charge rattling against a lamp post on the street. We lived in the suburbs, and a great crowd that had heard the shots gathered to see what was the matter. Dick told them simply that he had shot at a burglar.

We never knew positively who the mysterious one was that had frightened us so that night, but my father always thought it was a friend of his, who lived near us. Liddill had the reputation of being somewhat scary, and my father believed this friend threw the rocks at our house with the intention of playing a practical joke on Liddill, and to see how he would act. The theory seems all the more plausible because this friend came to our home very early the next morning and his face was unusually long and solemn. Whoever it was who threw the rocks had a narrow escape from being killed.

This dramatic scene of the shot fired through our door so suddenly and unexpectedly that night, will never fade from my memory. It is one of the earliest recollections of my life.

The first remembrance I have of my father, was after we had moved from Nashville to Kansas City, a short time after this adventure of Dick Liddill's. We lived in Kansas City, on East Ninth Street, between Michigan and Euclid; on Troost Avenue, between Tenth and Eleventh and on Woodland Avenue, between Twelfth and Thirteenth streets. I remember those different homes in an indistinct way, although I have often visited them since I grew up.

I remember very distinctly when we first came to Kansas City we lived for a short time with Charles McBride, who was married to my mother's sister. At that time there was a large reward for the capture of my father, and I suppose he thought it unsafe to leave us at McBride's on account of the well-known relationship, and that detectives might take a notion to look there for him. My father came one day, I remember, and moved us away. I asked him where we were going and he said, 'Ho another town." We went to the Doggett House, at Sixth and Walnut, and engaged rooms. We had been there only two or three days, when, as I was playing on the street in front of the hotel, I saw my uncle, McBride, pass on horseback and I shouted to him.

"Hello, Uncle Charlie! How did you get to this town?"

He spoke to me and rode on. When I went home and told my father about it, he at once paid his bill and took us away from there.

I have heard my folks tell since, that while we lived on Woodland Avenue, in Kansas City, there was a vacant lot behind our house, and the father of Con. Murphy, the County Marshall, lived on the other side of this lot. At that time Marshall Murphy was very anxious to capture my father and nearly every night a posse would gather at Murphy's house and start out for the country around Independence and in the "Cracker Neck" district in search of members of the James band. My father used to walk over to Murphy's house in the evening when the posse would be starting out, and talk to them about their plans, and wish them good luck on their trip. I told Mr. Murphy recently about this and he laughed heartily at it.

I remember seeing my father walking with a cane and limping, while we lived in Kansas City. I have been told since, that he did this, not because he was lame, but to help disguise himself.

My strongest Recollections of my father are of the times after we moved to St. Joseph, Mo. We went from Kansas City to St. Joseph in a covered wagon or "prairie schooner," drawn by two horses, and another horse, always saddled, leading behind. Charlie Ford drove the team. I sat most of the time on the seat with him, and father stayed inside the wagon until we were well out of Kansas City. We crossed the network of railroad tracks in the West Bottoms of Kansas City and drove up through Leavenworth and Atchison, Kan. It was my father's intention, when we started, to stop in Atchison and rent a house. When we reached Atchison we drove through the town and unhitched the horses at the edge of the town. Father and Charlie Ford rode back through the town to see if they could find a house for rent. They came back very soon and said the people were watching them suspiciously, so they hitched up again and drove on toward St.

Joseph. This suspicion of my father's was probably unfounded. He and Ford were undoubtedly stared at with the same degree of curiosity that any strangers on horseback would have been looked at. But at that time there was a big price on my father's head, and it would be strange if he was not suspicious. In St. Joseph we lived first in a house, the location of which I have forgotten. From there we went to the house on the hill where my father was killed.

It was while we lived in this house on the hill in St. Joseph that I best remember my father. I was then six years old. I remember my father as a tall, rather heavily built man, with a dark sandy beard. He was very kind to mother and to sister and to me. I remember best his good humored pranks, his fun making and his playing with me. I did not then know his real name or my own. I did not know that he was concealing anything from the public or that he was in danger of capture. He was living then under the name of Thomas Howard. My name was Charlie Howard, but my father and mother always called me "Tim." Father never called me by any other name than "Tim." Charlie Ford, who was at the house a good deal of the time, went by the name of Charles Johnson. They claimed to be cousins.

In those days in St. Joseph, father always kept at least two horses in the stable back of the house. Father was heavily armed at all times. In the house he kept a double barreled shot gun loaded with buckshot, a Winchester rifle, a 45-calibre Colt's revolver, a 45-calibre Schofield revolver, and three cartridge belts. He never left the house without both of the revolvers and the three cartridge belts loaded, and some cartridges in his pockets. That was the way he armed himself when he went down town. When he went away to be gone any length of time he carried in addition to this, a small valise full of cartridges. When on a trip h© carried his Winchester strapped on the inside of a large umbrella.

After my father's death we sold a great many of these things at public auction. The little cartridge valise brought $15. We did not sell the revolvers or cartridge belts. T. T. Crittenden, Jr. has one of the revolvers now, which I gave him as a token of my friendship for him. My uncle, Frank James, has the other revolver. Two of the cartridge belts were stolen from the house by the people who crowded in after my father's death. The third cartridge belt I have now and I shall always keep it in remembrance of my father.

At this same auction sale, after my father's death, we sold a little cur dog for $15. I felt the loss of the dog very much. The dog was given to my father by his half-sister, Mrs. Nicholson, when my father last visited my grandmother's home a short time before his death, and father brought the dog to St. Joseph with him. He rode in his arms on horseback.

My father was a great deal of the time at home while we lived in St. Joseph. He often took me with him for rides on horseback when the weather was fair. I generally rode in front of him, sitting astride of the horse's shoulders, and clinging with both hands to the mane. Sometimes I would ride behind him and hold on to his coat. These horseback trips led away out into the country beyond sight or hearing of the town. I recall very distinctly that on one of these trips he sat me up on top of a rail fence, where I hung on by the stakes, and then he rode away and showed me how he used to charge the enemy when he was a soldier under Quantrell. With the bridle rein in his teeth, and an unloaded revolver in each hand snapping the triggers rapidly, he charged toward me on the gallop, and I thought it was great fun.

One day the home of a preacher who lived in the suburbs of St. Joseph burned down, and the next day my father took me over on horseback to see the ruins. He talked quite awhile with the preacher and his wife. We found out after my father's death that this preacher used to live in Liberty, Mo., near the home of my people, and that both he and his wife recognized my father. But they kept the secret well. They could have earned the $20,000 by betraying my father, but they were loyal, as all friends of our family were in those days and in the trying times since then.

The spring my father was killed there was a great parade in St. Joseph in celebration of some public event. My father rode on horseback, with me in front of him, with the parade over its whole route. Leading the parade was a platoon of mounted police, and father rode right behind them.

One forenoon while my father was sitting at the window with me on his lap, he saw the chief of police of St. Joseph, and four men coming up the hill toward the house. Father got up hastily and sat me in a rocking chair, and told me to be very quiet. He ran out to the barn, and in a moment had his horse saddled. Then he came back into the house, and said a few words hurriedly to my mother while he put on his cartridge belts and revolvers, watching out of the window all of the time. He brought his Winchester rifle out of a closet and stood with it at the window, just far enough back so that the chief of police could not see him. The chief stopped in front of the house and put one foot and hand upon the fence as if to come in, and I saw my father take aim at him with the rifle. Then the chief evidently changed his mind and went away. In a moment more he would have been killed. My father thought of course that the chief had discovered who he was, and was coming after him. We learned after my father's death that the chief was simply showing some strangers over the city, and had brought them over the hill on which our house stood, because it overlooked the whole city.

My father used to hold me on his lap and talk a great deal to me about his adventures in th-e war. He used to talk to me about the James boys, and would read to me the accounts of their adventures that were published in the newspapers. He used to read to me from Major Edwards's book, stories about Quantrell's band of guerrillas, and show me the pictures. I have only hazy recollections of these things, of course, but I remember that once he showed me a picture of one of the members of the guerrilla band who was living then, and said laughingly, that he had a good long neck to hang by.

In days that father was lounging around the house, he often took the cartridges from his revolvers and buckled one of them around me, and strapped one with a handkerchief around my sister 's waist, and would say that I was Jesse James and that my sister was Sam Hildebrand. I remember well the name Sam Hildebrand, but I have never learned who he was, or if such a person ever lived.

My father was always heavily armed, and he told me that all the men went armed the same way. I thought that was true, because all the men I ever saw at our home were as heavily armed as he.

The morning my father was murdered we had just finished breakfast. I heard from the front room the loud roar of a shot. My mother rushed in and screamed. I ran in after her and saw my father dead upon the floor, and my mother was down upon her knees by his side and was crying bitterly. My father was killed instantly by the bullet that Ford shot into the back of his head. He never spoke or breathed after he fell.

Soon after the murder of my father a great crowd gathered outside the house. My childish mind imagined that these were responsible for the murder, and in great anger I lugged from its closet my father's shot gun and tried to aim it at the people outside, but my mother took it from me.

CHAPTER II. THE DEATH OF JESSE JAMES

The story of the murder of my father and the immediate events that led up to it I have learned since from my mother, my grandmother and others. Ten days before my father was killed, he and Charlie Ford and Bob Ford stayed all night at the home of my grandmother, Mrs. Samuels, near Kearney, Mo. My grandmother had known Charlie Ford for years, but this was the first time she had met his brother. Bob. She did not like the looks of Bob and she told my father that she did not believe Bob Ford was true. Father laughed at her and said:

"Mother, I don't set much store by him either, but he has got into some trouble and Charlie wants him to go with us till he can get a chance to leave the country. I'll keep my eye on him."

The last time that my father was at his birthplace was an ideal spring day. The grass and flowers were just coming up green and fresh, and the leaves were budding on the big coffee bean tree in the corner of the yard where he lies buried now. Father was in a good humor that day and he sat all of the afternoon with my grandmother in the shade of the porch and they talked together of old times. While they were sitting there a pretty red-headed woodpecker alighted on a tree fifty yards away and clung to the bark. My father pulled his revolver and said to my grandmother:

"Mother, have you heard about my being a good shot; I will show you."

He threw the revolver down on the little bird pulled the trigger and it fell dead.

My father was a wonderful marksman. I have heard his old comrades tell that seated on horseback with a revolver in each hand, he would ride at full speed between two telegraph poles, or two trees and begin firing at them when he was a few yards away, and before he was more than a few yards beyond them, he had emptied the chambers of both revolvers, and the six bullets from the revolver in his left hand were buried in the pole to the left of him, while the six bullets from the revolver in his right hand were in the pole to his right. I think this story of his marksmanship was true, because several different men in whom I have great faith told me they saw it done more than once. I have heard other stories of his great skill with his revolver that are equally as wonderful as this. I have seen my father at practice shooting with a revolver. That was while we were living at St. Joseph and when he had taken me on a horseback ride to a lonely part of the country. But I was too young then to pay much attention to it and I recall only that he was shooting at a mark on a tree.

After spending the day at the home of my grandmother, my father and the two Ford boys rode away on horseback to St. Joseph. Father carried with him a small dog that was given him by his half-sister as a present to my' sister and me. Father carried that dog in his arms all the way to St. Joseph.

The Ford boys killed my father for the reward that was offered for his apprehension. This reward was $5,000 for the apprehension of Jesse James and $5,000 additional reward for his conviction in any court. There has been a great deal of misunderstanding about this reward. It is generally believed that the reward was offered for the capture of Jesse James alive or dead. This was not the case. I have read the proclamation of Governor T. T. Crittenden offering the reward, and it was as I have stated.

The Ford boys had the confidence of my father. Charlie Ford had been with him off and on for years and father had befriended him and protected him and fed him when he was penniless. Father had not the slightest suspicion that the Fords meant to harm him.
This is proven by the fact that after breakfast that morning father took off his belt and revolvers and threw them upon the bed and threw his coat over them. He did this because it was a very warm morning and the belt and revolvers were tiresome to carry. Another reason was that it was necessary to have the doors and windows open, and father thought that people passing the house might be suspicious if they saw him armed.

After my father put the revolvers upon the bed he noticed that a picture on the wall was hanging awry. He placed a chair beneath the picture and stood upon it to straighten it and then he started to brush the dust from it. Standing thus, his back was turned to the Ford boys, who were in the room. This was the opportunity the Fords had been waiting for. It was the very first time they had seen him unarmed since they knew him. Bob Ford drew his revolver, aimed it at the back of my father's head and cocked it. Father heard the click of the hammer and made a movement as if to turn around. But before he could do so Ford pulled the trigger and father fell backward dead. The Fords ran out and across the back yard fence, and went down town and surrendered to the authorities, telling that they had shot and killed Jesse James. Years afterward the Fords, who found themselves despised of all men because of this murder, denied that they shot my father for the reward, but that they learned that Jesse James suspected them of treachery and meant to kill them, and they shot him for self protection. That this story was absolutely false is proven by the fact that immediately after the murder Charlie Ford sent the following telegram to the Governor of Missouri:

"I have got my man."

Charlie Ford practically admitted in my presence and hearing that he killed my father for the reward. That conversation was held under the following circumstances:

Nearly three years after the murder, when I was nine years old, I was in Kansas City with my grandmother. We were walking up Main street. I had hold of my grandmother's hand. Suddenly I saw and recognized Charlie Ford coming down the street toward us. I knew him the instant I saw him, and I was very much excited. I said to my grandmother:

"Here comes the man who killed my father."

It was the first time my grandmother had seen him since that day he was at her home with father, ten days before the murder. The sight of him made her weak and she sat down on a box in front of a shoe store. Ford saw her and went to walk past with his head turned the other way, but she called to him;

"You don't know me, Charlie?"

He stopped and said:

"Yes, I know you. You are Mrs. Samuels."

"Yes, and you killed my brave boy; you murdered him for money. I ought to kill you," she said to him.

He threw up both his hands in front of his face and answered: "Mrs. Samuels, don't say that. If you only knew what I am suffering, you wouldn't talk to me that way."

"And what have you made me and mine suffer?" she said.

"Mrs. Samuels, I have been in the blackest hell of remorse ever since it was done. But I didn't kill him. It was Bob did it," Ford said.

"Yes, and you knew Bob intended to do it when you brought him to my house. You ate bread under my roof with blackest murder in your heart, and murder for money, too. There will come a day of terrible reckoning for you. '

I heard Charlie Ford tell my grandmother in that talk that he did not know that Bob intended to kill my father till they got to St. Joseph, and then Bob told him if he did not consent to it, he would kill him along with Jesse. Ford repeated over and over again, that he was suffering the worst agonies of remorse. The perspiration streamed down his face and there were tears in his eyes. He begged my grandmother to forgive him and she said:

"If God can forgive you, I will.'"

My grandmother asked him what he did with the $10,000 he got for murdering my father, and he replied:

"Mrs. Samuels, before God, we never got but a few hundred dollars of that reward."

I watched Charlie Ford closely while he was talking. I was only nine years old but I understood it all. I said nothing until he had gone on down the street.

Then I said to my grandmother:

"If ever I grow to be a man I'm going to kill him."

My grandmother said to me:

"You'll never live long enough my son; God will never let an on very man like that live until then."

Eleven months after that day, Charlie Ford committed suicide in Richmond, Mo., by shooting himself. Bob Ford was shot and killed later in a gambling house in Colorado.

A great many persons have asked me in recent years if I would have sought revenge on the Fords if they had lived till I grew up. I have never given a direct answer to that question. I answer it now by saying that I would not have troubled the Fords or sought an encounter with them or any of the other enemies of my father. I realize that the feelings and prejudices of the days of border warfare have almost passed away, that the times and conditions have changed and that it was a certainty that with a price of $10,000 on his head it was only a matter of time till some traitor would kill my father to get it, and that if the Fords had not done it some other would have.

Every member of the James family has proven to the world in the seventeen years since my father's death that they are good citizens, and honest men and women.

The conditions and events and prejudices that led my father to become a member of Quantrell's guerrilla band, and the story of the persecutions and proscriptions that prevented his honorable surrender at the close of the war, and made him an outlawed and hunted man, are told of in the succeeding chapters.

CHAPTER III.THE JAMES FAMILY

My grandfather, Robert James, was a Baptist preacher of wide renown in the early days in Western Missouri. He was born and raised in Kentucky, and was a graduate of the Georgetown, Ky., college. His family was one of the old families of Logan County, Ky. My grandfather was married to my grandmother. Miss Zerelda Cole, one year before he graduated. He was then 23 years old, and she was 17. They met first at a religious gathering and it was a case of love at first sight. My grandmother's people lived in Lexington, Ky., and she was educated in a Catholic convent in that city. The Cole family, of which my grandmother was a member, was of old Revolutionary stock. Her grandfather was a soldier in the war of the Revolution. My grandmother's mother was a Lindsay, of the famous old Lindsay family of Kentucky. Senator Lindsay is a member of this family.

My grandfather and grandmother were married December 28, 1841. The following August they came to Clay County, Mo., to visit the mother of Mr. James, who had married her second husband and was living in that county. He left my grandmother in Clay County and returned to Kentucky. He was to have returned the next Christmas, but the Missouri river was frozen and he had to postpone the trip. He came in the spring. My grandfather liked Clay County and he remained there, settling near Kearney. He combined farming with preaching and was very successful at both. He acquired a large and valuable farm, on which my grandmother yet lives, and from the product of this farm he supported his family, because he never asked money for preaching and the good farmers to whom he broke the bread of life gave him very little. He was a great exhorter and a fervid expounder of the Gospel. He founded the Baptist churches at New Hope and at Providence, which are yet in existence. He was a wonderful revivalist and he baptized many of the old settlers of Clay County who are yet living and many more who are dead. I have had old men and women tell me of seeing him go into the water and baptize sixty converts at one time. At this time when my grandfather baptized sixty converts without leaving the water, my father, Jesse James, was fourteen months old, and he was held up in his mother's arms and saw the ceremony.

Years afterward, when my father had returned desperately wounded from the border wars, he was baptized not very far from the same place.

In 1851 my grandfather, the Rev. Robert James, went to California. The day he started, Jesse James was four years old. He clung to my grandfather and cried and pleaded with him not to go away. This affected my grandfather very much, and he told my grandmother that if he had not already spent so much money in outfitting for the trip, and if he had not promised the other men who were going with him, he would give up the trip. It was a great desire to get money to educate his children that led him to undertake the journey to the gold fields of California. My grandmother had a presentiment then that she would never see him again, and she never did. The overland trip from Clay County to California lasted from April 12 to August 1, three months. My grandfather lived only eighteen days after reaching California, and was buried there.

He had preached the gospel for eight years and received in all that time less than $100 for his services. He was a good Christian and a" noble man.

The children of my grandfather were:

Alexander James, born January 10, 1844.

Robert James, born July 19, 1845, died in infancy.

Jesse W. James, born September 5, 1847, died April 3, 1882.

Susan L. James born November 25, 1849, married November 24, 1870, to Allen H.

Palmer, died 1889.

My grandmother remained a widow for four years. She married Dr. Reuben Samuels in 1855.

The children born of that marriage were:

Sarah L. Samuels, born December 26, 1858, married November 28, 1878, to William Nicholson.

John T. Samuels, born May 25, 1861, married July 22, 1885, to Norma L. Maret.

Fannie Quantrell Samuels, born October 18, 1863, married December 30, 1880, to Joseph Hall.

Archie Payton Samuels, born July 26, 1866, murdered by Pinkerton detectives, January 26, 1875.

My grandmother had eight children. Two of them were murdered.

My grandmother lives yet on the old homestead near Kearney, Mo. Dr. Samuels, her second husband, lives with her, but is old and quite feeble. My grandmother is seventy-four years old, is vigorous and in good health.

CHAPTER IV. THE BORDER WARS

The Kansas Jayhawkers and Red Legs made the Missouri guerrilla possible. When the civil war broke out, Eastern Kansas was filled with abolitionists who formed themselves into marauding bands, called Jayhawkers and Red Legs, who invaded Western Missouri, ostensibly in the interests of the Union cause, but really for the purpose of plunder, making war an excuse for robbery. Jackson and Clay Counties were settled mostly by people of Southern sympathies, many of them from Kentucky. The marauding bands from Kansas stole and drove off horses and cattle, enticed negro slaves away, robbed and burned houses, hanged and shot men and insulted women. These outrages led to the organization of the Missouri guerrillas under Quantrell.

Charles William Quantrell was born in Hagerstown, Md., in 1836. In 1855 Quantrell came to Kansas and joined his only brother and they/started on a trip overland to California, with a negro as cook and hostler. Although there was peace at that time, Western Missouri and Kansas were at war. Armed bands which called themselves "patriots" roamed over Kansas and made frequent dashes into Missouri. One night in the summer of 1856, when the Quantrell brothers were camped on the Little Cottonwood river, on the way to California, one of these bands of thirty-two armed men rode deliberately up and attacked the little camp. The elder Quantrell was killed instantly and Charles William Quantrell was left for dead. But he did not die. He lay in great agony for two days, scarcely able to move, keeping the coyotes and buzzards from the body of his brother. Early in the morning of the third day an old Shawnee Indian found and rescued Quantrell and buried his dead brother, and nursed Quantrell back to life.

The experiences and sufferings of those two awful days and nights made a fiend of Quantrell. When he recovered he taught school long enough to pay the old Indian for his board and then he went to Leavenworth, and under the name of Charles Hart, he joined the Jayhawkers. He was promoted to the position of orderly sergeant, and held the esteem and confidence of all. But it was revenge he was after, and he bided his time. In the four years he was with the Jayhawkers, he killed thirty out of the thirty-two men who had' murdered his brother, and each one of them was shot mysteriously in the very center of the forehead. Quantrell was discovered by his comrades at last and then he fled '"to Jackson County, Mo., and organized Quantrell's band of guerrillas.

Major John N. Edwards says of Quantrell:

"One-half of the country believes Quantrell to have been a highway robber crossed upon the tiger; the other half that he was the gallant defender of his native South; one-half believes him to have been an avenging nemesis of the right; the other a forbidding monster of assassination. History cannot hesitate over him, however, nor abandon him to the imagination of the romancers. He was a living, breathing, aggressive, all-powerful reality— riding through the midnight, laying ambuscades by lonesome roadsides, catching marching columns by the throat, breaking in upon the flanks and tearing a suddenly surprised rear to pieces; vigilant, merciless, a terror by day and a superhuman if not a supernatural thing when there was upon the earth blackness and darkness."

Major Edwards, in his wonderful book, "Noted Guerrillas, or the Warfare of the Border," speaks thus of the men who formed the guerrilla band under Quantrell.

"As strange as it may seem, the perilous fascination of fighting under a black flag—where the wounded could have neither surgeon nor hospital and where all that remained to the prisoners was the absolute certainty of speedy death—attracted a number of young men, born of higher destinies, capable of sustained exertion in any scheme or enterprise and fit for callings high up in the scale of science or philosophy. Others came who had deadly wrongs to avenge, and these gave to all their combats that sanguinary hue which yet remains a part of the guerrilla's legacy. Almost from the first, a large majority of Quantrell's original command had over them the shadow of some terrible crime. This one recalled a father murdered, this one a brother waylaid and shot, this one a house pillaged and burned, this one a relative assassinated, this one a grievous insult while at peace at home, this one a robbery of all his earthly possessions, this one the force which compelled him to witness the brutal treatment of a mother or sister, this one was driven away from his own like a thief in the night, this one was threatened with death for opinion's sake, this one was proscribed at the instance of some designing neighbor, this one was arrested wantonly and forced to do the degrading work of a menial; while all had more or less of wrath laid up against the day when they were to meet face to face and hand to hand, those whom they had good cause to regard as the living embodiment of unnumbered wrongs. Honorable soldiers in the Confederate army —amenable to every generous impulse and exact in the performance of every manly duty—deserted even the ranks which they had adorned, and became desperate guerrillas because the home they left had been given to the flames, or a gray-haired father shot upon his own hearth-stone. They wished to avoid the uncertainty of regular battle and know by actual results how many died as propitiation or a sacrifice. Every other passion became subordinate to that of revenge. They sought personal encounters, that their own handiwork might become unmistakably manifest. Those who died by other agencies than their own were not counted in the general summing up of a fight, nor were the solacements of any victory sweet to them unless the knowledge of being important factors in its achievements. As this class of guerrillas increased, the warfare of the border became necessarily more cruel and unsparing. Where at first there was only killing in ordinary battle, there became to be no quarter shown. The wounded of the enemy next felt the might of his individual vengeance—acting through a community of bitter memories—and from every stricken field there began, by and by, to come up the substance of this awful bulletin: Dead such and such a number, wounded none. The war had then passed into its fever heat, and thereafter the gentle and the merciful, equally with the harsh and revengeful, spared nothing clad in blue that could be captured."

At the outbreak of the civil war my people lived near Kearney, in Clay County, Mo. My grandmother being a native of Kentucky was naturally a Southern sympathizer, as was her husband. Dr. Samuels.

In that neighborhood at that time were a great many sympathizers with the Northern cause. Many of these had formed themselves into organizations known as "Home Militia" or "Home Guards" and these often operated in conjunction with the raiders from Kansas who came into Missouri to pillage and kill. Members of these organizations hated my grandmother because she was a Southern sympathizer and outspoken in her loyalty to the cause of the Confederacy.

The feeling in those days was very intense against Southern sympathizers. Northern spies in Southern uniforms would go to families and get a drink of water or something to eat, and the families would be persecuted for it and sometimes put in jail.

In the spring of 1863 a band of Northern militiamen came to the home of my grandmother and demanded to know where Quantrell was. Quantrell's band had been in that neighborhood shortly before this, and these militiamen thought, I suppose, that my folks could be frightened into telling where they were, if they knew. My father was sloughing corn with Dr. Samuels when the militiamen came up. They took Dr. Samuels from the plough and drove him at the points of their bayonets to a tree near the barn and put a rope around his neck and hung him to a limb until he was nearly dead. Then they lowered him, loosened the rope, and demanded that he tell where Quantrell was. He did not know and of course could not tell. He would not have told if he had known. Three times they strung him up to the limb and lowered him. The rope cut into his neck until it bled.

The militiamen drove my father, who was a boy of fifteen, up and down the corn rows, lashing his back with a rope and threatening him with their bayonets. They forced him up to the mulberry tree to witness the cruel treatment of his stepfather.

When they were through torturing Dr. Samuels with the rope, they went to the house and pointing their guns as my grandmother, said:

"You had better tell what you know."

My grandmother answered: "I am like Marion's wife, what I know I will die knowing."

Captain Culver was commanding the squad of militiamen. He shouted to the men under him, who were at the rear of the house with Dr. Samuels:

"Bring him around here and let him bid his wife good bye."

My grandmother asked him what he intended doing with her husband.

"I'm going up here to kill him and let the hogs eat him, " was the reply.

They took him away and had been gone a short while, when three shots were heard in the direction they had gone. My grandmother thought they had killed him, and believed so for days afterward. But they did not kill him. They rode with him until midnight and lodged him, hungry and suffering great pain with his neck, in the jail at Liberty.

After the militiamen had gone with his stepfather, Jesse James said to his mother:

"Ma, look at the stripes on my back."

My grandmother took off his shirt, and his back was livid with long stripes. My grandmother wept at the sight and he said to her:

"Ma, don't you cry. I'll not stand this again."

"What can you do?" she asked him.

"I will join Quantrell," he said.

"But they have stolen all the horses, and you have no money, " she said.

"Time will bring both," was the reply of my father.

Soon after this my grandmother and her daughter were arrested and taken to St. Joseph and thrown into jail, and kept there twenty-five days. No charge was made against her. She was imprisoned in this shameful way simply because she and her sons were Southern sympathizers. Is it to be wondered at that her sons, beaten, imprisoned, tortured, persecuted at every turn, and driven from home joined Quantrell's avenging band?

That same spring after Jesse James had been beaten by the militiamen, Fletcher Taylor, a member of Quantrell's guerrillas, and one of the most desperate fighters the world ever saw, came for him and took him to join Quantrell.

The exciting life and the horseback riding with Quantrell agreed with my father. He had been a delicate boy, but in one winter he grew so stout and strong that when he returned home the following spring for a short visit, his mother did not know him at first. Fletcher Taylor came home with him on that visit. He said to my grandmother:

"You didn't know the boy, did you?"

"No, I did not," his mother said.

Taylor pointed to my father and said:

"There is the bravest man in all Quantrell's command."

"Yes, anyone would be brave if they had done to them what the militiamen did to him," was the answer my grandmother made to this.

In his book, "Noted Guerrillas, or Warfare of the Border," Major Edwards says of the causes that drove my father to be a guerrilla:

"His mother and sister were arrested, carried to St. Joseph and thrown into a filthy prison. The hardships they endured were dreadful, often without adequate food, insulted by sentinels who neither understood nor cared to learn the first lesson of a soldier —courtesy to women—cut off from all communication with the world, the sister was brought near to death's door from a fever which followed the punishment and the mother— a high spirited and courageous matron— was released only after suffering and emaciation had made her aged in her prime. Before she returned to her home Jesse had joined the dreaded Quantrell.

"Jesse James had a face as smooth and as innocent as the face of a school girl," says Major Edwards in his book. The blue eyes—very clear and penetrating—were never at rest. His form—tall and finely moulded—was capable of great effort and great endurance. On his lips there was always a smile, and for every comrade a pleasant word or a compliment. Looking at the small, white hands with their long, tapering fingers, it was not then written or recorded that they were to become with a revolver among the quickest and deadliest hands in the West. Jesse's face was something of an oval. He laughed at many things. He was light hearted, reckless, devil may care. He was undaunted."

CHAPTER V. JESSE JAMES AS A GUERRILLA

Whether or not my father was in the Lawrence raid I am unable to say. I have heard some of his comrades say that he was there and some of them say he was not there. Jesse James was at Centralia, September 27, 1864. A train from St. Louis reached there at 11 o'clock that morning having on board twenty-four Federal soldiers. Quantrell's guerrillas were there to meet it. As the train slowed up the soldiers looked out of the windows and saw the waiting guerrillas on the platform. One of the federals recognized Bill Anderson, one of Quantrell 's bravest men, and said to his comrades:

"'Lord! Lord! There is Bill Anderson! Boys, go to praying."

Bill Anderson's sisters had been killed by Federal soldiers, and over their dead bodies he had sworn a solemn oath to never spare a Federal, and he never spared one. When he was killed the silken cord on which he tied a knot each time he killed a Federal soldier had fifty-four knots on it.

The twenty-four soldiers were taken off the train stood in line and shot.

Later in the day, Major Johnson and three hundred Federal soldiers went three miles southeast of Centralia and attacked the two hundred and sixty-two guerrillas who were encamped there in the timber. The guerrillas came out to meet them. The story of the fight is best told by Major Edwards and it is a true account of it, as follows:

"Major Johnson halted his men and rode along his front speaking a few calm and collected words. They could not be heard in the guerrilla ranks, but they might have been divined. Most battle speeches are the same. They are generally epigrammatic, and full of sentences like these: 'Aim low,' 'keep cool,' 'fire when you get loaded,' 'let the wounded lie till the fight is over. 'But could it be possible that Johnson meant to receive the charge of the guerrillas at a halt? What cavalry books had he read? Who had taught him such ruinous and suicidal tactics? And yet monstrous as the resolution was in a military sense, it had actually been taken, and Johnson called out loud enough to be heard from opposing force to opposing force: 'Come on, we are ready for the fight.'

"The challenge was accepted. The guerrillas gathered themselves up together as if by a sudden impulse, and took the bridle reins between their teeth. In the hands of each man there was a deadly revolver. There were carbines also, and yet they never had been slung. The sun was not high, and there was great need to finish quickly whatever had need to be begun. Riding the best and fastest horses in Missouri, the guerrillas struck the Federal ranks as if the rush was a rush of tigers. Jesse James, riding a splendid race mare, led by half a length, then Arch Clements, then Peyton Long, then Oil Shepherd. There was neither trot nor gallop; the guerrillas simply dashed from a walk into a full run. The attack was a hurricane. Johnson's command fired one volley and not a gun thereafter. It scarcely stood until the interval of three hundred yards was passed over. Johnson cried out to his men to fight to the death, but they did not wait even to hear him through. Some broke ranks as soon as they had fired and fled. Others were attempting to reload their muskets when the guerrillas, firing right and left, hurled themselves upon them. Johnson fell among the first. Mounted as described, Jesse James singled out the leader of the Federals. He did not know him then. No words were spoken between the two. When Jesse James reached to within five feet of Johnson's position, he put out a pistol suddenly and sent a bullet through his brain. Johnson threw out his hands as if trying to reach something above his head and pitched forward heavily, a corpse. There was no quarter. Many begged for mercy on their knees. The guerrillas heeded the prayer as a wolf might the bleating of a lamb. The wild rout broke away toward Sturgeon, the implacable pursuit, vengeful as hate, thundering in the rear. Death did its work in twos, in threes, in squads—singly. Beyond the first volley, in which three were killed and one mortally wounded, not a single guerrilla was hurt.

"Probably sixty of Johnson's men gained their horses before the fierce wave of the charge broke over them, and these were pursued by five guerrillas, led by Jesse James, for six miles at the dead run. Of the sixty, fifty-two were killed on the road from Centralia to Sturgeon. Todd drew up his command and watched the chase go on. For three miles nothing obstructed the vision. Side by side over the level prairie the five stretched away like the wind, gaining step by step and bound by bound, upon the rearmost riders. Then little puffs of smoke arose. No sounds could be heard, but dashing ahead from the white spurts terrified steeds ran riderless. Night and Sturgeon ended the killing. Five men had shot fifty-two. Johnson's total loss was two hundred and eighty-two, or out of three hundred only eighteen escaped. History has chosen to call this ferocious killing at Centralia butchery. In civil war encounters are not called butcheries when the combatants are man to man and where over either rank there waves a black flag. Johnson's overthrow, probably, was a decree of fate. He rushed upon it as if impelled by a power stronger than himself. He did not know how to command, and his men did not know how to fight. He had, by the sheer force of circumstances, been brought face to face with two hundred and sixty-two of the most terrible revolver fighter the American war or any other war ever produced, and he deliberately tied his hands by the act of dismounting, and stood in the shambles until he was shot down. Abject and pitiful cowardice matched itself against reckless and profligate desperation and the end could only be just what the end was. The guerrillas did unto the militia just exactly what the militia would have done unto them if fate had reversed its decision and given to Johnson what it permitted to the guerrillas.

Father was with Todd a few days after Centralia when they made a raid from their camp on the Black water into Lafayette County to break up a German Federal military organization. The militia knew Todd and his guerrillas were coming and they formed an ambuscade of one hundred men in some hazel brush near the road and sent fourteen cavalrymen down the road to meet the guerrillas, and to fire upon them and to fall back past the ambush. Jesse James and ten men rode ahead of the main body of one hundred and sixty-three guerrillas. These ten men met the fourteen cavalrymen and charged them, driving them past the ambuscade. Todd and his one hundred and sixty-three guerrillas heard the firing in front and rushed up, and his command received the fire from the ambush full in the teeth. Todd and his men dismounted and rushed into the brush and killed all but twenty-two of the one hundred militiamen hiding there. While this was going on Jesse James and the ten guerrillas with him had killed ten of the fourteen cavalrymen farther down the road and were pursuing them when they ran at full speed into the advance of a Federal column two hundred strong. There was nothing for the eleven guerrillas to do but turn and run for dear life pursued by the two hundred Federals shooting and yelling. My father's splendid race mare, that had borne him so well in the Centralia fight, was killed beneath him. Father was shot in the left arm and side. He fell behind his dead horse and fought from there, shooting down five of the Federals closest to him. The balance of the guerrilla company came up at this critical time and drove off the Federals. In this day's fight one hundred and seventeen militia were killed and Jesse James killed ten of them.

There is not room in a book of this size to tell one-hundredth part of the adventures, the comings and goings, the hot battles, the victories and the hairbreadth escapes of Quantrell's guerrilla band, of which my father was a member. Only a few of these events, in which my father took a prominent part will be mentioned here.

The attack of Plattsburg, Mo., by the guerrillas was one of these most thrilling events. The court house in the center of the square in Plattsburg was held by forty-six Federal soldiers heavily armed. Twelve guerrillas marched to the town in the night. Three hundred yards from the square they formed fours and made a charge forward. The garrison in the court house was warned of their coming, and every window was full of guns, and the square was swept by mini balls. The twelve guerrillas attacked the court house in the face of a pitiless fire and captured it. Forty-six Federal soldiers surrendering to twelve guerrillas, who broke to pieces the two hundred muskets they found in the court house and appropriated $10,000 in Missouri defense bonds they found there. The forty-six Federal soldiers were paroled under sacred promise that in the future they would treat non-combatants and Southern sympathizers with more mercy than they had done in the past.

Leaving Plattsburg, the guerrillas crossed the Missouri river to Independence. Four miles from Independence there was a disorderly house kept by several women, and it was a resort for the officers of the Federal garrison at Independence. The guerrillas set a trap to catch these officers.

Jesse James, dressed as a young girl, rode on horseback up to this house and called its mistress out. Imitating the voice and manner of a girl my father told her that he lived not far away, that he was a girl fond of adventure, and would like to come to the house that night, bringing two or three neighbor girls, "to have a good time." The mistress of the house consented, and the supposed girl on horseback said he and the other girls would be there that night.

The mistress sent word at once to the Federal officers in Independence that four new girls would be at her house that night.

It was after dark when Jesse James and the other guerrillas rode up to the house, and dismounting, crept up and peered in at the windows. Twelve Federal officers were in there with the women. No guards or sentinels were out. The Federals felt secure. All the company was in one room, five women and twelve men. A cheery fire blazed and crackled on the hearth of the old-fashioned fire place.

Jesse James, with five men, went to one window. Bill Gregg, with four men, went to another. Each of the nine guerrillas in the darkness outside selected his man. At a signal that had been agreed upon there was a crack of nine revolvers that sounded like the discharge of a single gun. The glass, shivered in a thousand bits, crashed, and nine of the Federal soldiers fell dead at that first volley. The remaining three fell dead an instant later. The guerrillas mounted and rode away.

The next fight of these guerrillas was in June, 1863. Todd led the command of seventy guerrillas, and the plan was to capture and burn Kansas City. But on the way to Kansas City these seventy guerrillas met in the old Santa Fe trail near Westport a column of two hundred Federals. These were soldiers from Kansas, on their way to Kansas City. Todd drew his men up in line and said to them:

"These Kansas soldiers are the fellows we want. They had better be fought out here in the open than behind brick walls."

Todd formed his men behind a knoll near Brush Creek, and himself rode forward to reconnoiter the advancing column. The signal for the guerrillas to advance was when Todd lifted his hat. Todd mounted on a superb horse, stood in the middle of the road and watched the advancing Federal column. At the proper moment he turned to the knoll behind him and lifted his hat, at the same time hitching his revolvers around to his front. The seventy guerrillas came over the hill and galloped down like a whirlwind into the faces of the two hundred soldiers who were a part of the Ninth Kansas cavalry under Capt. Thatcher. It was a hot day. The dust rose in clouds from under the hoofs of the horses and rolled above them. The battle was a hand to hand conflict. The guerrillas with their bridle reins in their teeth and a big revolver in each hand rode right into the Column, firing with the right and left hand at once and never missing a man. In this fight my father, although he was only a boy, won this remarkable compliment from old Bill Anderson:

"For a beardless boy he is the keenest and cleanest fighter in the command."

Eighty Federals were killed before their column wheeled in a mad, clattering rout back to the Kansas prairies they had just left. The seventy guerrillas chased them, firing and killing as they went. The fleeing Kansas cavalry ran straight into a solid regiment of the Federal infantry and formed behind it. The guerrillas had to retreat but they had lost only three men.

After this the guerrillas were unusually active. Eight of them came upon eight Federals and drove them into a barn and then set it on fire and as the eight soldiers ran out to escape the flames each was killed in turn.

Twelve guerrillas came to a tavern west of Westport, in Kansas, and killed eight Federal soldiers who were stopping there.

Todd, with ten guerrillas, met eighteen Kansas Red Legs on the road to Independence, and killed fifteen of them.

Poole and thirty guerrillas hid in the woods on a hillside that overlooked a spring on the road three miles west of Napoleon. Eighty-four Federal cavalry came along and stopped there to water their horses. Thirty-three of the eighty-four Federal cavalry were killed and eleven badly wounded.

Jesse James was in all of these combats.

In July, 1863, Major Ransom and four hundred Federals, with two pieces of artillery were met on the road between Blue Springs and Pleasant Hill by twenty guerrillas under Todd, who was one of Quantrell's lieutenants. The twenty guerrillas made a whirlwind charge into the ranks of the four hundred Federals and killed fifteen of them and wounded a dozen, and then fell back, and kept charging and then retreating down the road. Ransom pursued slowly, firing his cannon from every hill top. Quantrell's full command joined Todd and formed in line of battle beyond a ford of the Son that Ransom would have to pass. Quantrell charged down upon the Federals as they were crossing this ford and forced Ransom to retreat to Independence, leaving seventy-three of his men dead behind him.

Anderson, one of Quantrell's officers, and twenty guerrillas, circled Olathe, Kay, and killed thirty eight Federal infantry they found in a foraging party.

After the Lawrence raid, in which the guerrillas killed a number of Kansans variously estimated to be between one hundred and forty-three and two hundred and sixteen, the Federals began scalping the guerrillas they killed in fair and foul fights. There had been no scalping before that. The first body scalped was that of Ab. Haller, a guerrilla of great courage and fighting energy. He was hiding, desperately wounded, in so-me timber near Texas Prairie, near the eastern limits of Jackson County. Seventy-two Federal soldiers found him there and demanded his surrender. But a guerrilla never surrendered at any time or place. Desperately wounded as he was, Haller, single handed and alone, fought from the brush the seventy-two soldiers and killed five of them before they succeeded in killing him. In the fight he was wounded eleven times. The fatal bullet went fair through his heart. His slayers were so infuriated at the gallant fight he made that they scalped him and cut off his ears. An hour or two later the body was found by Andy Blunt and a small party of guerrillas. When they saw the mutilated body of their brave comrade they took this oath:

"Hereafter it is scalp for scalp."

Thereafter a few of the more desperate guerrillas scalped their victims, and a few of the Federals did the same. But in truth it must be said that most of the guerrillas and most of the Federals never mutilated a body. My father never did this, it is needless for me to say, and he disapproved of it most emphatically, but a few of the guerrillas had been desperately and shamefully wronged by the Kansas militia, and when they saw the bodies of their dead comrades mutilated they took an eye for an eye and a tooth for a tooth.

There is not space here to tell of the many savage combats that occurred between guerrillas and Federals all over Jackson, Clay and Lafayette Counties in Missouri, and Johnson

County in Kansas, in these years of the war. The guerrillas were not always cruel. Sometimes they were merciful. An instance of this was when a company of guerrillas surrounded eleven Federals in a house of ill repute four miles west of Wellington in Lafayette County. The Federals were ordered to come out and they came. Ten of them were shot down. The eleventh could not be found. A search of the house was made and he was found dressed as a woman in one of the beds. He had hoped by this ruse to escape. This soldier fell upon his knees when he was discovered and begged piteously for his life. He promised, if he was spared, to desert the army and throw his gun away and go home to his mother. He prayed and wept. When he talked about his mother, and begged to be spared for her sake, Arch Clements, the most desperate of them all, took pity on him and said to him:

"Come, get up off your knees and go outside with me."

Arch Clements led him out into the woods under the shade of a huge oak near the roadside.

"For the sake of my dear mother do not kill me," he begged. He was almost a boy, with a fair, honest face. Clements halted him under the oak tree, out of sight of his guerrilla comrades and said to him, pointing down the road:

"You are free; go, and go quick."

The Kansas boy ran out into the darkness, and Clements discharged his pistol in the air and returned to his comrades, who believed that the pistol report they heard had sent a bullet through the young man's heart.

My father was badly wounded and almost killed August 13, 1864, at Flat Rock Ford, over Grand river. Sixty-five guerrillas were camped there. A mile away lived a northern sympathizer who notified a body of Federals. Three hundred militia and one hundred and fifty Kansas Red Legs under Col. Catherwood were guided up to the foot of a ravine, where they dismounted and crept up to within range of the guerrillas before the Federals were discovered. Jesse James and Peyton Long saw the Federals first and gave the alarm. Bill Anderson, who was in command, shouted clear and loud:

"Hurry up, men; half of you bridle up and saddle up the horses, while the other half stand off the devils."

The guerrillas answered with a cheer. While half of them were saddling the horses the others formed in the rush and with an incessant and unnerving revolver fire kept the four hundred and fifty Federals at bay. As soon as the horses were ready the guerrillas leaped into their saddles and charged the Federals. Sixty-five men against four hundred and fifty, but those sixty-five were whirlwind fighters and not one of them ever knew what it was to be afraid of anything. That charge was a death grapple. Peyton Long and Arch Clements fell each with a horse killed. Anderson and Tuck Hill each went down with slight wounds. Jim Cummings took Anderson up behind him, Oil Shepherd picked up Arch Clements and Broomfield took up Peyton Long, but Long's revolver was shot from his hand. Broomfield's horse was shot beneath him. Jesse James, Cave Wyatt, William Reynolds and McMacane charged clear through the four hundred and fifty Federals and then charged back again. Dock Rupe, a boy of seventeen, fell dead alongside of Jesse James.

My father fell next, just as he was leading a third charge upon the Federals. He was hit twice. The first wound made him reel in his saddle and his pistol dropped from his right hand. He recovered himself and drew another pistol with his left hand and fired 'several shots. But a Spencer rifle ball struck him in the right breast, tore a great hole through the lung and came out his back near the spine. No man could bear up under such a wound as that. My father fell. Arch Clements sprang to his side and was standing over him fighting, when Clements was shot again in the face and again in the left leg and fell beside my father.

The desperate and bloody grapple went on. Never did a handful of men fight against such terrible odds. The whole Federal force, cut to pieces by the guerrillas charges, retreated to heavy timber and reformed there, leaving behind seventy-six killed and one hundred wounded. The guerrillas took advantage of this to get away, taking every one of their wounded with them. This they did in all their fights. A wounded guerrilla was never left behind, because the Federals showed no quarter to even wounded guerrillas. My father was sent to the home of Captain John A. Rudd, in Carroll County, and Gooly Robertson, Nat Tigue, Oil Shepherd and Peyton Long were detailed to guard him with their lives. It was not thought that my father would live through the night. Bill Anderson kissed him fondly as he parted with him, and my father, who did not think he had long to live took from his finger a plain gold ring and gave it to Peyton Long to be delivered to his sister Susie.

My father was nursed to life and strength by Mrs. Rudd and Mr. and Mrs. S. Neale.

The guerrillas who were in this desperate fight escaped with a loss of five or six and scattered out to reunite at an appointed rendezvous.

The success of the guerrillas in such encounters as this at Flat Rock Ford was due to their own peculiar training, tactics and methods of fighting. The guerrillas were trained, as Major Edwards has said, "solely in the art of horseback fighting. To halt, to wheel, to gallop, to run, to swing from the saddle, to go at full speed horseback, to turn as upon a pivot—to do all these things and to shoot either with the right hand or the left while doing them—this was guerrilla drill and guerrilla discipline. Taking the first Federal fire at a splendid rush, they were to stop for nothing. No matter how many saddles were emptied, the survivors—relying solely upon the revolver—were to ride over whatever stood against the whirlwind or sought to check it in its terrible career."

In September, 1864, my father had recovered from the terrible wounds he had received in the fight, at Flat Rock Ford. He left the Rudd home against the earnest protests of his nurses and physician, who said he was not strong enough to travel; crossed the Missouri river on a raft, and joined Todd in Jackson County. He was thin and pale as a ghost. Jesse James was in Todd's camp near Bone Hill when General Sterling Price sent Capt. John Chestnut to Todd with a communication asking Todd, who was operating with Quantrell, to gather up all the guerrillas he could and stir up the militia in North Missouri.

Price was then preparing for his Missouri campaign. Todd immediately sent my father to Dave Poole in Lafayette County with orders to gather up his men at once. This order was executed and my father returned to Todd, who sent him with eleven men under Lieut. George Shepherd to cross the river into Clay County to harass the militia there. These men could not find a boat, and they crossed the river in an old horse trough, using fence rails for oars. Todd crossed the river a few days later. He surprised forty-five militia in camp and killed them all. The guerrillas went to Keytesville, which was held by a garrison of eighty militia. Todd and his men surrounded the fort and the eighty militiamen surrendered without firing a shot. The prisoners were paroled.

A few days later Todd's command came upon one hundred and fifty Federal soldiers escorting seventeen wagons. Ninety-two of the one hundred and fifty were killed. In this fight my father, as he galloped on horseback, killed a Federal lieutenant two hundred yards away. The lieutenant had just lifted his carbine to his face when a bullet from my father's heavy dragoon pistol crushed into his head. This remarkable shot was the talk of the command for a long time thereafter.

This battlefield was described afterward in the following language:

"The scene after the conflict was sickening. Charred human remains stuck out from the moldering wagon heaps. Death, in all forms and shapes of agony made itself visible. Limbs were kneaded into the deep mud of the roadway, and faces, under the iron feet of the horses, crushed into shapelessness."

The march against Fayette began the morning of September 30, 1864. The town was reached at eleven o'clock that forenoon and the attack began at once. Four hundred Federal soldiers were garrisoned there. Todd had two hundred and seventy seven men altogether. The Federals were behind such strong fortifications that they repulsed the guerrilla attack. When the guerrillas retreated Lee McMurtry was left wounded under the shadow of the stockade. Todd called for volunteers to bring him out. My father and Richard Kinney returned and ran in under a heavy fire from the stockade and carried McMurtry out to safety. McMurtry is now sheriff of Wichita County, Texas.

The guerrillas under Poole joined General Price in his famous Missouri raid and remained with him, scouting and picketing and fighting with the advance until Price started Southward from Mine Creek. After Mine Hill they returned to Bone Hill, Jackson County, some going afterward into Kentucky with Quantrell, and some to Texas with George Shepherd. From that time on the days of the guerrillas in Missouri as an organized band were over.

CHAPTER VI. CLOSING DAYS OF THE BORDER WARFARE

After the death of Todd, near Independence and the retreat of General Price from Missouri, the guerrilla band was broken up. Lieut. George Shepherd, taking with him Jesse James, Matt Wayman, John Maupin, Theo. Castle, Jack Rupe, Silas King, James and Alfred Corum, Bud Story, Perry Smith, Jack Williams, James and Arthur Devers, Press Webb, John Norfolk, James Cummings, William Gregg and his wife, Dick Maddox and his wife, James Hendrick and his wife, and others to the number of twenty-six, started south from Jackson County to Texas, November 13, 1864.

November 22, 1864, Shepherd and his twenty-six veterans were riding southward on Cabin Creek, in the Cherokee nation. They met Capt. Emmet Goss of Jennison's old command, riding northward with thirty-two Kansas Jayhawkers. My father had a special grievance against Goss, who was six feet tall and had red hair and was a desperate fighter. My father had encountered him before and had sworn to kill him if he ever met him again. When the two commanders lined up and charged each other my father rode straight for Capt. Goss. Goss fired at' him point blank four times while my father was trying to control his horse, which became unmanageable in the melee, owing to the fact that my father was suffering with a wound in his left arm. My father got close to Goss at last and shot him through and through. Goss reeled in his saddle but held on and refused to surrender. My father fired again and killed him. Of the thirty-two Kansans, twenty nine were killed and only three escaped.

At Sherman, Texas, Shepherd disbanded his men December 2 and took a part of them into Western Texas. My father and seven others remained to take service with Arch Clements and the remainder of Bill Anderson's guerrillas.

March 1, 1865, Clements and his command started on a march for old Missouri again. They had many fights and skirmishes on the way and after they got into Missouri.

March 14, 1865, the guerrillas in Missouri held a conference to talk over a plan of surrender. The Confederate armies everywhere had surrendered, with the exception of Shelby's brigade, which was going into Mexico to espouse the cause of Maximilian. The guerrillas at this conference decided to surrender, with the exception of Clements, Jesse James and several others, and bearing a flag of truce, they marched into Lexington, Mo., to allow all who wanted to surrender to do so. My father rode at the head of the column and bore the white flag of truce. They held a conference with Major Rodgers and were marching out again, my father yet in front carrying aloft the white flag, when eight Federal soldiers fired point blank at them and were charged in turn by the guerrillas and routed. Four of the Federals were killed and two wounded. These eight who had charged the guerrillas were the advance of a body of sixty Federals, thirty Johnson County militia and thirty of the Second Wisconsin cavalry. A Wisconsin trooper singled my father out and charged him. At the distance of ten feet both fired together and my father's dragoon pistol bullet went through his heart. Another Wisconsin trooper charged my father, firing as he came. My father killed his horse and the trooper sent a pistol ball through my father's right lung, the same lung that had been torn through by a bullet not so long before at the Flat Rock Ford fight. My father fell and his horse fell dead on top of him. As the Federals galloped past, five of them fired at my father as he lay pinned to the ground. My father pulled himself from beneath the horse and ran for the timber. Five Federals pursued him firing as they ran. My father turned once and at a distance of two hundred yards killed the Federal who was leading the chase. This caused a momentary halt of his pursuers, and during it he pulled off his heavy cavalry boots which were nearly full of blood. Before he started again to run in his stocking feet he fired at his pursuers and shattered the right arm of one of them. The other three Federals were pressing him close. My father was getting weaker and weaker from loss of blood. The leader of the three pursuers yelled at him:

"Damn your soul, we've got you at last. Stop and be killed like a gentleman."

My father, at bay, tried to lift his heavy dragoon pistol but was too weak to lift it with one hand alone. He grasped it in his two hands and killed the Wisconsin trooper who had cursed him.

The remaining one of the five turned and ran. My father staggered five hundred yards further and fell fainting upon the bank of a creek.

This encounter occurred March 15, 1865. That night, the next day and all of that night and till sunset of the third day, my father lay alone on the banks of the creek, bathing his wound and drinking the water. He had a burning fever, and the bullet hole through his lung gave him the most intense pain. At sunset of March 17, he crawled to a field where a man was ploughing and this man proved to be a friend of the Southern cause. This new-found friend carried my father on horseback that night to the home of Mr. Bowman, a distance of fifteen miles. There my father was tenderly nursed by his inseparable companion Arch Clements, till the surrender of Poole, March 21, with one hundred and twenty nine guerrillas. It was well understood by these guerrillas and also by Major Rodgers to whom they surrendered, that my father was considered one of the number who surrendered, although his wounds kept him from actually surrendering. Major Rodgers understood this so well, and he was so fully convinced that my father would die, that he thought it unnecessary to parole him when he paroled the other guerrillas, and Major Rodgers declared then that this was why he did not parole him, because he thought it an unnecessary formality to go through with in the case of a dying man.

I have gone thus into detail about this because it has been published thousands of times and is generally believed, that my father did not surrender at the close of the war. He did surrender, and surrendered in good faith. The attack upon him and the handful of guerrillas with him when they were returning with a white flag after negotiating the terms of surrender with the proper official, shows how bitter was the prejudice against the guerrillas. It was a prejudice that developed into a persecution most cruel and which prevented my father from surrendering or from living at home, and which made him a hunted man, with a price on his head, for sixteen long years and finally caused his murder. Arch Clements refused absolutely to surrender on any terms; he preferred to fight to the death.

To enable my father to reach his mother, who had been banished by Federal militia from her home in Clay County, to a home among strangers in Nebraska, Major Rodgers furnished my father with transportation, money and a pass on a steamboat.

To show how genuine was the surrender of my father, and that the Federal forces thereabouts looked upon it as genuine, I will state, as a matter of fact, that while waiting at Lexington for a steamboat up the Missouri river, my father became acquainted with the soldier who had shot him through the lung. He was John E. Jones, Company E, Second Wisconsin cavalry. My father and he became fast friends and exchanged photographs.

At the time of this surrender my father had the scars of twenty-two wounds on his body.

At this point I will quote again from the writings of Major John N. Edwards, that faithful historian of the guerrilla warfare of the border. He says in extenuation of the things the guerrillas did.

"Was it justifiable? Is there much of anything that is justifiable in civil war? Two civilizations struggled for the mastery, with only that imaginary thing, a state line, between them. On either side the soldiers were not as soldiers who fight for a king, for a crown, for a country, for an idea, for glory. At the bottom of every combat was an intense hatred. Little by little there became prominent that feature of savage atrocity which slew the wounded, slaughtered the prisoners, and sometimes mutilated the dead. Originally the Jayhawkers in Kansas had been very poor. They coveted the goods of their Missouri neighbors, made wealthy or well-to-do by prosperous years of peace and African slavery. Before they became soldiers they had been brigands, and before they destroyed houses in the name of retaliation they had plundered them at the instance of individual greed. The first Federal officers operating in Kansas that is to say, those who belonged to the state—were land pirates or pilferers.

"Stock in herds, flocks, droves and multitudes, were driven from Missouri into Kansas. Houses gave up their furniture; women their jewelry; children their wearing apparel; storerooms their contents; the land its crops; the banks their deposits. To robbery was added murder, to murder arson, and to arson depopulation. Is it any wonder, then, that the Missourian whose father was killed should kill in return? Whose house was burned should burn in return? Whose property was plundered should pillage in return? Whose life was made miserable, should hunt as wild beast and rend accordingly? Many such were in Quantrell's command—many whose lives were blighted; who in a night were made orphans and paupers; who saw the labor and accumulation of years swept away in an hour of wanton destruction; who, for no reason on earth save that they were Missourians, were hunted from hiding place to hiding place; who were preyed upon while a single cow remained or a single shock of grain; who were shot at, outlawed, bedeviled and proscribed, and who, no matter whether Union or Disunion, were permitted to have neither a flag nor a country."

While quoting on this subject from the writings of Major Edwards, I wish to use one more extract from them, which gives Major Edwards' estimate of Cole Younger. He says:

"The character of this man to many has been a curious study, but to those who knew him well there is nothing about it of mystery or many sideness. An awful provocation drove him into Quantrell's band. He was never a bloodthirsty or a merciless man. He was brave to recklessness, desperate to rashness, remarkable for terrible prowess in battle; but he was never known to kill a prisoner. On the contrary there are alive today fully two hundred Federal soldiers who owe their lives to Cole Younger, a man whose father had been brutally murdered, whose mother had been hounded to her death, whose family had been made to endure the torment of a ferocious persecution and whose kith and kin, even to most remote degrees were plundered and imprisoned. At Lawrence he was known to have saved a score of lives; in twenty other desperate combats he took prisoners and released them; when the steamer Sam Gaty was captured, he stood there a protecting presence between the would-be slayers and their victims at Independence he saved more lives; and in Louisiana probably fifty Federals escaped certain death through Younger's firmness and generosity. His brother James did not go into the war until 1864, and was a brave, dauntless, high-spirited boy who never killed a soldier in his life save in fair and open battle. Cole was a fair-haired, amiable, generous man, devoted in his friendships, and true to his word and to comradeship. In intrepidity he was never surpassed. In battle he never had those to go where he would not follow, aye, where he would not gladly lead. On his body to-day there are scars of thirty six wounds. He was a guerrilla, and a giant among a band of guerrillas, but he was one among three hundred who only killed in open and honorable battle. As great as had been his provocation, he never murdered; as brutal as had been the treatment of every one near and dear to him, he refused always to take vengeance on those who were innocent of the wrongs and who had taken no part in the deeds which drove him, a boy, into the ranks of the guerrillas, but he fought as a soldier who fights for a cause, a creed an idea, or for glory. He was a hero and he was merciful.

"John Thrallkill, another of Quantrell's band, who fought with Jesse James along all the border side, was a Missourian turned Apache. He slept little; he could trail a column in the starlight; his only home was on horseback, and he had already mixed with the warp and woof of his young life the savage agony of tears. Thrailkill, when the war began, was a young painter in Northwest Missouri, as gentle as he was industrious. Loving a beautiful girl, and loved ardently in return, he left her one evening to be absent a week. At its expiration they were to be married. Generally the woman who is loved is safe, but this one was in peril. Her father, an invalid of fifty, was set upon by Federal militia and slain, and the daughter, bereft of her reason at the sight of the gray hairs dabbled in blood, went from paroxysm to paroxysm, until she too was a corpse. The wildest of her ravings were mingled with the name of her lover. It was the last articulate thing her lips lingered over or uttered. He came back as a man in a dream. He kissed the dead reverently. He went to the grave as one walks in his sleep. It was bitter cold and someone remarked it to him. 'Is it,' he said; 'I had not felt it.' Another friend, tried to fashion something of a solacement. The savage intensity of the answer shocked him: 'Blood for blood; every hair in her head shall have a sacrifice!' The next day John Thrailkill began to kill. He killed over all Northwest Missouri; of the twenty militia who were concerned in the murder of his sweetheart's father and indirectly in the murder of his sweetheart; he killed eighteen.

William Anderson was another of Quantrell's men who had a wrong to avenge. He was a strange man. If the waves of the civil war had not cast him Tip as the avenger of one sister assassinated and another maimed, he would have lived through it peacefully, the devil that existed in him sleeping on, and the terrible powers latent there remaining unaroused. It is probable that he did not know his own nature. He certainly could have not anticipated the almost miraculous transfiguration that came to him on the eve of his first engagement—that sort of transfiguration which found him a stripling and left him a giant.

"He was a pensive, brooding, silent man. He went to war to kill, and when this self-declared proposition was once well impressed upon his followers, he referred to the subject no more. Generally those who fought him were worsted; in a majority of instances annihilated. He was a devil incarnate in battle, but had been heard over and over again to say: "If I cared for my life I would have lost it long ago; wanting to lose it I cannot throw it away." And it would appear from the history of his career up to the time of his death, that what in most men might have been regarded as fatalism was but the inspiration of a palpable destiny Mortal bullets avoided him. At desperate odds fortune never deserted him. Surrounded, he could not be captured. Outnumbered, he could not be crushed. Surprised, it was impossible to demoralize him. Baffled by adversity, or crippled and wrought upon often by the elements, he wearied no more than a plough that oxen pull, or despair never so much as the granite mass the storms beat upon and the lightnings strike. Shot dead from his saddle at last in a charge reckless beyond all reason, none triumphed over him a captive before the work was done of the fetters and the rope. His body, however, remained in the hands of the enemy, who dragged it for some distance as two mules might draw a saw log, and finally propped it up in a picture gallery in Richmond, Mo., and had pictures taken of the wan, drawn face of the dead lion and his great mane of a beard that was full of the dead leaves and the dust of the highway."

CHAPTER VII.AFTER THE WAR

During the war my grandmother, Mrs. Zerelda Samuels, was banished from her home in Clay County by the Home Guards. These Home Guards were Northern sympathizers whose chief business it was to harass and torment people living in the same neighborhood who were Southerners. As a sample of the persecutions of these "patriots" I have heard my grandmother tell that once during the war, when my father was with Quantrell, a band of Home Guards came to her home and after plundering the barn came to the house and began nosing around. One of them said to my grandmother:

"Just show me a southern man and I'll show you a thief."

My grandmother noticed hanging from beneath his overcoat the straps of a bridle of hers that he had just stolen from the barn. She pointed to it and asked sternly:

"What is that you have under your coat?"

"0h, that is only a bridle that I pressed into the service," he replied.

"'Well, I will just press you/' my grandmother said, and she grabbed him and backed him up into a corner and choked him until he was blue in the face and his tongue hung out. One of his comrades ran to the door and yelled:

"Help! help!"

One of his comrades up by the barn shouted the inquiry:

"'What's the matter down there?"

"Mrs. Samuels is choking Sam to death," was the answer.

A month or two after this happened this same soldier returned to my grandmother's house. She saw him coming and threw a shovel full of hot coals from the fireplace into his face and he ran away.

My grandmother was warned by these Federal soldiers to leave Clay County and to go South, "where she belonged," or she would be killed. She went away but she did not go South. My father told her not to go South, because, he told her, when the war closed times would be so hard she would find it difficult to get North again, and if she did finally get back to Clay County she would find some Kansas Jayhawker squatted on her place. So my grandmother and her family moved North. She was first imprisoned in the jail at Weston for two days. Then she was released on her promise to leave the country. She hired a man to drive her to Nebraska and paid him $1 a mile for eighty-five miles. She and her family went in an open wagon in the bitter winter weather of February. The sleet often froze on her and her two little children as they drove northward. She went to Rulla, Neb., and her husband practiced medicine there.

When my father surrendered at the close of the war so badly wounded with a bullet through his lung that he could scarcely walk, he went on a steamboat from Lexington, Mo., up the Missouri river to my grandmother at Rulla, Neb. Richard West, one of Quantrell's guerrillas went with him and cared for him on the way. He reached Rulla in April. He stayed there with my grandmother eight weeks, and in that time he was often so near death that my grandmother would bend over his bed and put her ear to his heart to see if it was yet beating. One day at the end of eight weeks he drew the face of his mother down to his and said to her:

"Ma, I don't want to be buried here in a Northern state."

"My son, you shall not be buried here," my grandmother told him.

"But, ma, I don't want to die here."

"If you don't wish to you shall not, " my grandmother told him, and at once she announced to the members of her household:

"We are going back to old Missouri if the trip kills every one of us. Jesse don't want to die here."

She began preparing immediately for the trip and the very next day my father was put aboard of a boat bound down stream. He was so weak and sick that four men carried him to the boat as he lay on a lounge. He fainted while they were carrying him to the boat, and the people of Rulla tried to persuade my grandmother to abandon the trip. But she would not listen to it. Her son wished to die on Missouri soil and that was enough for her.

On the steamboat my father recovered consciousness enough to ask:

"Ma, where am I?"

"On the boat, honey, going home," my grandmother told him.

"Thank the Lord," he said, and fainted again.

The trip down river seemed to help him a little. He was landed at Harlem, across the river from Kansas City, and was carried to the home of John Mimms, who kept a boarding house there.

He was wounded so badly that for months he could not even sit up in bed. He was nursed by Zerelda Mimms, my mother, and his sister, Susie James, she nursed him from early August till late in October, and then he was strong enough to be moved and he begged to be taken to his old home near Kearney. "When he left it was agreed between him and Miss Zerelda Mimms that if ever he recovered, they would be married.

He was carried home in a wagon. When he reached home he could not walk a step. After a week or two of nursing he could walk across the room and used to say to my grandmother:

"Ma, if I only get so I can walk through the whole house I will be happy."

At that time his wounds discharged so that at stated intervals he had to lean over and allow the pus to drain into a vessel.

He did not tell his mother of his engagement to marry until he was strong enough to ride out a little on horseback. Then he said to her one day:

"Ma, I am going to marry Zee."

My grandmother was opposed to him marrying anyone and she told him so, but he replied in a way that convinced her and silenced all her opposition to it:

"Ma, Zee and I are going to be married."

As soon as my father was strong enough to get around he attended a revival service held in the Baptist church in Kearney and was converted and confessed religion, and was baptized and joined the church. His was a sincere conversion. No one who is acquainted with the life and doings of my father will accuse him of hypocrisy in this act because a hypocrite is a coward, and even the worst enemy my father ever had never accused him of cowardice. He would not stoop to hypocrisy to convince his enemies that his surrender at the close of the war was sincere and that his only wish was to live a clean, honest, God-fearing life, and at peace with all the world.

But the hatred of the Southern people that rankled in the hearts of the Northern militia and home guards during the war did not die down at its close. They yet hated the Southern soldiers who had honorably surrendered. Even in his desperately wounded condition my father was not permitted to stay at home. He was warned by friends and threatened by enemies.

One night while he was sleeping upstairs at the home of his mother the family was aroused by the sound of signal whistles outside, as if someone was calling and answering. My father got painfully out of bed and crawled to the window and looked out. He saw six horses tied to the fence in front of the house and he saw that they had on United States government saddles and he divined instantly that they were Home Guards. He got the heavy dragoon pistols he had carried through the war and came down stairs and said to his mother:

"Ma, the house is surrounded, but don't be scared, I have been in tighter places than this and come out all right. I will fight my way out."

The six men came upon the front porch and demanded the surrender of Jesse James. He asked them through the door what they intended to do with him.

"Hang you, by God, " their leader answered.

Thereupon my father, sick and weak as he was, threw open the front door, and, with pistol in each hand stepped out on the porch, and the six armed Home Guards backed away as the wounded Jesse James advanced, and finally broke into a run, regained their horses and galloped away. One printed account has it that my father killed three or four of the Home Guards that night, but this is untrue.

My father knew well that after this repulse the Home Guards would return with a larger gang and would surely kill him if he stayed at home. So that very night he mounted a horse and rode away. There was snow on the ground and it was a bitter cold night. It was the night of February 18, 1867. He made a long ride that night to the house of a friend. His enemies were searching for him everywhere, however, and they kept him dodging around. This caused his wound to open again and he became so ill that he could not be moved. He was hiding in a house in the timber and Dr. Woods attended him and nursed him so well that in the spring he was able to travel to New York City, and there he took steamer and went to California by way of the Isthmus of Panama. He went to the home of his uncle, Woodson James, who owned a hotel near a hot spring of wonderful medicinal qualities and there he stayed for a year, and then returned quietly to his mother's home in Clay County, hoping that in that time the old prejudices and hatreds had died down and that he would not be molested if he stayed close to home and worked the farm for his mother.

But he had been home but a short time when his old enemies, the Home Guards, smelled him out and came after him again. There had been a bank robbery in Gallatin, Mo., and one of the robbers, in escaping, had narrowly missed being killed, and had left behind a horse that had once been the property of my father. This horse had been sold by my father to James Anderson, a brother of Bill Anderson. But it was identified as having once belonged to Jesse James and that gave his persecutors a chance to accuse him of the robbery and to swear out a warrant for his arrest. Sheriff Thomason and a posse went to my grandmother's house to arrest my father, who knew full well that if they ever got hold of him they would kill him. Jesse James was at home when the posse came, and saw them in time to get out the kitchen window at the rear of the house and run to the barn for his horse. The posse saw him as he mounted and they chased him up through the pasture. When he thought he had gone far enough he turned in his saddle and shot the sheriff's horse dead and warned the posse that the first man who came a step nearer would be shot in his tracks. They knew he would do as he said and they returned to the house, and Sheriff Thompson took out of the barn my father's favorite horse Stonewall, and rode him away. My father returned in a few minutes, and when he found they had stolen his horse it made him very angry. He started after the whole posse but they got away. He rode on to Kearney and there he wrote a letter to the sheriff and mailed it, telling him that he did not wish to kill him because he had been a Southern soldier, but if he did not return Stonewall to his stall before the end of three days there would be trouble sure enough. Two days later the horse was returned and Sheriff Thomason never tried to arrest my father again.

This incident forced my father to leave home again. That night he went to the home of General Jo Shelby, in Lafayette County, and stayed there six weeks. At the end of that time he became homesick. General Shelby sent Dave Poole, a veteran ex-guerrilla, to my grandmother's house to test the loyalty of the negro servants and see if it would be safe for my father to return. Neither my grandmother nor the servants knew Poole. My grandmother had two servants, Ambrose, called "Sambo," and Charlotte. Both had been slaves in our families from their birth, and when freedom came to them with the Emancipation Proclamation they refused to accept it, preferring to remain at the old home, and they spent the rest of their days there and died there.

Poole came to the house pretending to be a detective. He first went to the barn where

Sambo was currying the horses, and shoved a big revolver Up against his face, and backing him into a corner demanded:

"Tell me where Jesse James is or I'll blow your damn brains out."

"I can't tell you, boss. I haven't seen him," the negro answered, and he stuck to it.

Poole then went to the house and put a revolver to Charlotte's face and demanded:

"Now tell me where Jesse James is or I'll kill you. "

"Why, I haven' seen him since the war," she replied.

Poole went back to General Jo Shelby's and reported that the negroes were true blue. My father went home and almost the first thing he said to my grandmother was:

"Ma, don't ever let Aunt Charlotte and Ambrose want for a thing as long as you have a crust of bread."

Old Aunt Charlotte was a sincere Christian, and the falsehood she had told Poole worried her considerably and she asked my grandmother if she thought God would mark down the lie against her.

"No, my dear; you will wear a crown in glory for that," my grandmother told her.

My father was home only a short time when the home guards smelled him out again and drove him away. From that time to the day of his death, fourteen years later, he was a hunted and an outlawed man.

As a fitting close to this chapter I will quote again from the book by Major John N. Edwards, "Noted Guerrillas, or the Warfare of the Border." This book was published in 1877, and has long been out of print. It is a graphic and faithful account of the doings of the guerrillas and some of the happenings in Western Missouri immediately after the war. In this book Major Edwards says:

"To the great mass of the guerrillas the end of the war also brought an end to their armed resistance. As an organization they never fought again. The most of them kept their weapons; a few had great need of them. Some were killed because of the terrible renown won in the four years war; some were forced to hide themselves in the unknown of the outlying territories; and some were mercilessly persecuted and driven into desperate defiance and resistance because they were human and intrepid. To this latter class Jesse James belonged. No man ever strove harder to put the past behind him. No man ever submitted more sincerely to the result of a war that had as many excesses on one side as on the other. No man ever went to work with a heartier good will to keep good faith with society and make himself amenable to the law. No man ever sacrificed more for peace, and for the bare privilege of doing just as hundreds like him had done—the privilege of going back again into the obscurity of civil life and becoming again a part of the enterprising economy of the commonwealth. He was not permitted to do so, try how he would, and as hard, and as patiently.

"Jesse James, emaciated, tottering as he walked, fighting what seemed to everyone a hopeless battle of 'the skeleton boy against skeleton death'—joined his mother in Nebraska and returned with her to their home near Kearney, in Clay County. His wound would not heal, and more ominous still every once in a while there was a hemorrhage. In the spring of 1866 he was barely able to mount a horse and ride a little. And he did ride, but he rode armed, watchful, vigilant, haunted. He might be killed, waylaid, ambuscaded, assassinated; but he would be killed with his eyes open and his pistols about him. The hunt for this maimed and emaciated guerrilla culminated on the night of February 18, 1867. On this night an effort was made to kill him.

"Jesse James had to flee. In those evil days bad men in bands were doing bad things continually in the name of law, order and vigilance committees. He had been a desperate guerrilla; he had fought under a black flag; he had made a name of terrible prowess along the border; he had survived dreadful wounds; it was known that he would fight at any hour or in any way; he could not be frightened out of his native state; he could be neither intimidated nor robbed; and hence the wanton war waged upon Jesse James, and hence the reason why today he is an outlaw, and hence the reasons also that—outlaw as he is and proscribed in county or state or territory—he has more friends than the officers who hunt him; and more defenders than the armed men who seek to secure his body, dead or alive.

Since 1865 it has been pretty much one eternal ambush for this man—one unbroken and eternal hunt twelve years long. He has been followed, trailed, surrounded, shot at, wounded, ambushed, surprised, watched, betrayed, proscribed, outlawed, driven from state to state, made the objective point of infallible detectives, and he has triumphed. By some intelligent people he is regarded as a mythic; by others as in league with the devil. He is neither, but he is an uncommon man. He does not touch whiskey or tobacco in any form. He never travels twice the same road. He never tells the direction from which he came nor the direction in which he means to go. There is a design in this—the calm, cool, deadly design of a man who recognizes the perils which beset him and who is not afraid to die. He trusts very few people, two probably out of every ten thousand. He comes and goes as silently as the leaves fall. He never boasts. He has many names arid many disguises. He speaks low, is polite, deferential and accommodating. He does not kill save in stubborn self defense. He has nothing in common with a murderer. He hates the highwayman and the coward. He is an outlaw, but he is not a criminal, no matter what prejudiced public opinion may declare, or malignant partisan dislike make noisy with reiteration. The war made him a desperate guerrilla, and the harpies of the war—the robbers who came in the wake of it, and the cut-throats who came to the surface as the honorable combatants settled back again into civilized life—proscribed him and drove him into resistance. He was a man who could not be bullied—who was too intrepid to be tyrannized over —who would fight a regiment just as quickly as he would fight a single individual—who owned property and meant to keep it—who was born in Clay County and did not mean to be driven out of Clay County—and who had surrendered in good faith, but who, because of it, did not intend any the less to have his rigs and receive the treatment the balance of the Southern soldiers received. This is the summing up of the whole history of this man since the war. He was hunted, and he was human. He replied to proscription by defiance, ambushment by ambushment, musket shot by pistol shot, night attack by counterattack, charge by counter-charge, and so he will do, desperately and with splendid heroism, until the end."

The foregoing was written by Major Edwards in 1877, five years before my father's death.

CHAPTER VIII.OUTLAWED AND HUNTED

For sixteen years of his life, beginning within 1866 and ending April 3, 1882, when he was killed, my father was outlawed, and police officials and detectives were searching for him everywhere, except in the right place to find him. In these long years he had many thrilling adventures, some amusing ones, and many narrow escapes none of which have ever been told in print before. Owing to the fact that my father had only two photographs ever taken and that these were in the hands of his family and were never seen by those who were searching for him, no correct picture of him was ever printed and consequently his features were unknown to all except a few, and nearly all of these were loyal friends who could be depended on never to betray him under any circumstances. My father used to live in Kansas City and other cities, and go and come on the busiest streets in broad daylight, as any other citizen would, even when a large reward was offered for his capture. Of course he was in great danger of discovery at all times, and he was always heavily armed.

While the officers were hunting for him at one time there was an agricultural county fair held in Kansas City, and among the prizes offered was one for the best lady's saddle horse, which must be shown in action before the judges at the fair. My father attended this fair and entered his favorite horse, "Stonewall," for the prize. In the competition for the prize "Stonewall" was ridden by Miss Annie Ralston, and the horse took first prize. At that very moment there was a big reward offered for my father's capture.

At another time my father entered a horse in the races at the Jackson, Miss., fair. The race was in three heats. My father was quite sure that his was a better horse than any in the race, but in the first heat he failed to win. My father suspected that the jockey was holding the horse in deliberately and for the purpose of making him lose the race, so my father himself rode the horse in the last two heats and won the race and the purse.

A year or two after the close of the war my father and a companion who had been with him in Quantrell's command, were riding on horseback through the mountain districts of Tennessee. They stopped for dinner at a house along a country road and while resting there learned that the woman of the house was a widow whose husband had also been a guerrilla with Quantrell, and had died a short time before of wounds received in one of the skirmishes of the last days of the war. My father noticed that the widow was very despondent, and he supposed it was because of the death of her husband. He talked to her in a consoling way, and she told him that what worried her most just then was that her house and little farm was mortgaged for five hundred dollars, the loan fell due that very day, and she expected the sheriff and the money-lender to come that afternoon and foreclose the mortgage and order her off the place. My father had fought in the same company with her husband in the war. He had five hundred dollars with him, but it was about all he did have, and he was a stranger in a strange land and could not spare the money. But he was determined to aid the widow of his old comrade in some way. He said to her:

"Suppose you had the five hundred dollars to pay the money lender when he came, would you know how to sign up the papers and get your receipts all correct so there would be no flaw in it?"

She told him she did. He then gave her five hundred dollars, with instructions to be very particular to see that the mortgage was taken up. My father inquired from her the road by which the sheriff and mortgagee would drive out, and then he and his companion bade the woman good-bye and rode away. But they did not go far. They dismounted not far from the widow's home, and led their horses into the brush and concealed themselves. They saw two men go past in a buggy driving in the direction of the widow's home. In an hour or two when these two men came driving back over the same road they were halted by my father and his companion.

"Are you sheriff so and so?"

"Yes."

"And money-lender so and so?'"

"Yes."

"Throw up your hands."

"The sheriff and the money-lender obeyed and were relieved of the five hundred dollars, and then were told to drive on. This act of my father's was certainly open to criticism, but by it the widow's home and farm were saved to her and my father regained the money which he had to have to continue his journey. I give this as an example of how desperate chances Jesse James would take to aid the widow of a comrade in distress.

In the later years of his life my father stopped at the home of General Jo Shelby in Lafayette County, to rest himself and his horse from a long journey. General Shelby had a negro boy whom he thought a great deal of. This boy was a waif of the war who had drifted into General Shelby's camp during the war to get something to eat, and Shelby had adopted him. This boy had gone that day to a near-by town with a load of firewood to sell. On a former trip to town this negro boy had been set upon and beaten by the white boys of the town, and this time he took with him an old army pistol that he had taken from the General's room. When he reached town the boys set upon him again, and the negro boy pulled out his pistol and shot one of them in a leg. The wounded boy ran away howling, and the other boys followed him. The negro boy knew that the white folks would get after him for this, so he hurriedly unhitched his mules, mounted one of them and started on a run for General Shelby's house. He was within a mile of the house when a posse of white men on horseback hove in sight on his trail. The boy urged his mule into a faster run, and had just reached the gate at the foot of the lane leading to General Shelby's house when the mob caught him and dragged him from the mule and started away with him.

My father had taken one of General Shelby's shot guns and was out beyond in a pasture hunting quail when he saw the mob ride up to the gate. He very naturally supposed that the mob had discovered that he was there and had come after him. He went on a run for the stable to get his horse, but before he reached there he saw the mob riding away with the negro boy.

General Shelby was not at home, but his wife was there and she was almost distracted when she saw the mob capture her negro boy and ride away with him. My father declared that he would go and rescue the boy. She begged him not to do it. But he felt in duty bound, as the guest of his friend General Shelby, to protect his servants in his absence, so he saddled his horse and went on a gallop after the mob. There were more than a dozen men in the mob. My father overtook them as they had halted on a high bridge over a creek and was getting ready to lynch the young negro. All of these men were armed, but my father rode right in among them and demanded:

"What are you going to do with that boy?"

"Lynch him," answered a dozen men in chorus.

"What has he done?"

"He shot a white boy. The niggers are getting too bold and we're going to make an example of this one."

"No, you are not," my father said. "That is General Shelby's boy and I am General Shelby's friend. If that boy has harmed a white man he must have a fair trial for it."

The argument might have lasted longer and become more pointed and animated but a man in the mob recognized my father and exclaimed:

"That's Jesse James."

The men in the mob grew respectful at once and asked what had better be done.

"The best thing for you to do is to take this boy to Lexington and turn him over to the sheriff and have him put in jail, and let him get the same sort of a fair trial that a white boy would get. That will satisfy General Shelby, it will satisfy me, and it ought to satisfy you."

The men in the mob agreed to it and went to Lexington and did as agreed. My father rode behind them to the outskirts of Lexington, and then rode away.

The negro boy was tried by a jury and acquitted. Henry Clay Campbell was a soldier in Marmaduke's brigade of Price's army. He surrendered at Shreveport, La., and returned to his former home in Cooper County, Mo. A man who lived four miles from Butler, in Bates County, owed Campbell $1,000 since before the war, and at the close of the war Campbell went there to collect the debt. This man who owed him had been a soldier in the Federal army, and when Campbell came to collect the $1,000 this rascal set a gang of fifteen Federal soldiers upon him to kill him. These soldiers, on horseback, were pursuing Campbell, who was also on horseback, along a country road. My father, Arch Clements, Oil Shepherd, and two others saw the pursuit and they ambushed themselves near the road, and as the Federals rushed by six of them were shot and killed and the rest gave up the chase of Campbell and escaped.

As narrow an escape as my father ever had from capture was in the 70's when he and a companion were riding through Jackson County one warm day in August. They had been riding all day were tired and dusty when they came to the Little Blue river, and decided to halt there and take a plunge bath. They tied their horses in the brush, undressed and left their clothing on the bank and plunged into the water. They were in the water up to their necks and were talking to each other, and never dreaming of danger, when suddenly from the bank came the stern command:

"Throw up your hands."

Jesse James and his companion turned their heads quickly, and there on the bank was standing a man with a double-barreled shot gun to his shoulders and the two muzzles pointing fair at the men in the water. There was nothing for the two naked men to do but to obey the command, and up went their hands. It was the first and only time my father ever put up his hands at the command of anyone, and it was the first and only time that he was ever captured. This time he was caught sure enough. His clothing and revolvers were on the river bank behind the determined looking man with the shot gun.

"Come out here,' was the next command.

There was not time to form a plan of operation. But my father and his companion were used to surprises and to the necessity of quick action. Experience together in different "tight places" had sharpened their wits so that each almost divined what was going on in the mind of the other, and without either having spoken a word to the other they acted in concert on a plan of escape.

At the command of the man behind the shot gun my father waded slowly ashore, talking and arguing all the time with the man on the bank to distract and confuse him. The other man stayed in the water with his hands above his head, watching father and the man with the shot gun. My father walked up the bank, demanding earnestly all the while to know why two gentlemen enjoying a quiet bath after a day's horseback ride should be disturbed in this rude manner.

As soon as my father reached the side of the man on the bank, his companion, who was in the water, gave a shrill war whoop and dived beneath the surface. This shrill yell so surprised and disconcerted the man with the shot gun that he turned his head quickly away from my father, and looked at the man in the water. That was the chance my father had been waiting for. Quick as a flash he sprang upon the man, grabbing his shot gun and him at the same time, and they rolled over in the weeds locked together in a fierce wrestling match. They had hardly grappled each other before the man in the water was out and got hold of one of his own revolvers and the rest of it was easy.

The man turned out to be a country constable who was out hunting for horse thieves. He came upon the two horses in the brush and jumped at the conclusion that the two men in the water were horse thieves, and determined to capture them. He never once suspected who the men really were that he had captured. My father dipped his shot gun in the water so it could not be fired, took away all his ammunition and gave him a good ducking in the Blue and let him go his way.

My grandmother was greatly harassed in these times by detectives who came to her home searching for my father. She learned to suspect every stranger who came there, and to be very wary in her talks with them. At one time during the war Fletcher Taylor and eight guerrillas who were traveling through Clay County near her home were very tired and hungry. They knew of only one house to which they might safely go and ask for food, and that was my grandmother's. Taylor had been there before with my father, and he supposed, of course, that my grandmother would recognize him and it would be all right. It was late at night when he and his eight companions rode up to the house and knocked at the door. My grandmother inquired from within:

"Who is there?"

"It is Fletcher Taylor and eight guerrillas, Mrs. Samuels; we are very hungry."

In those perilous times Federal soldiers often went in the guise of guerrillas to the homes of Southern patriots and asked for food or water, and if it was given them the people who gave it were reported and punished for giving aid and sustenance to the rebels. So my grandmother was very suspicious and cautious.

"I don't know you," she said. "Go away and do not bother me."

"But I am Fletcher Taylor, who was here with your son Jesse."

"That is a good lie. I never saw or heard tell of Fletcher Taylor," she answered.

"But don't you remember, Mrs. Samuels, the good gooseberry pie and clean pair of socks that you gave me."

My grandmother knew then that it was all right and she threw open the door and prepared a meal for the hungry soldiers.

One time after the war my father was at home and was lying on the floor reading a book, when his mother discovered three men coming up on horseback. She called to my father; he got up and looked out the window and saw that it was the sheriff. He went out the back door, and as he went my grandmother said to him:

"My dear boy, if it is necessary fight till you die. Do not surrender."

She gave him that advice because a little before that time two men who had been with Quantrell were arrested and put in jail at Richmond, and a mob had taken them out and hanged them.

My father got to his horse and was so closely chased that he had to turn in his saddle and shoot the collar off the sheriff's neck. That ended the pursuit.

Among the many cruel falsehoods that have been told and retold, and printed and reprinted about my father, is that he murdered Whicher, a Pinkerton detective, near my grandmother's home and then carried the body to the banks of the Missouri river, fourteen miles distant, and ferried it across the river and left it in Jackson County. Some writers have embellished this story and made it the more horrible by telling that my father hobbled the detective first and started him to running and then shot at him as he ran, clipping off pieces of his flesh; and that after the man was dead, my father sliced off his ears and carried them around in his vest pocket.

This story is absolutely false; and not only that, it is so ridiculous that any one would know it was false who cared to look at it in a fair way. It is a fact that Whicher was found dead in Jackson County, twenty miles or .more from my father's home and on the other side of the river. He had simply been shot without any mutilation. If he had been shot near my father's home, is it likely that whoever killed him would have gone to the trouble of carrying the body away across to where it was found? It would have been much easier to have buried the body where it was killed.

That story of Whicher's killing was concocted by Pinkerton detectives, who knew my father had no hand in the killing. The man who killed Whicher is living in Texas today.

Pinkerton's detectives, in the pursuit of my father and their harassment of my grandmother, were guilty of as wanton and cruel a murder as was ever done anywhere. I can deny that my father ever killed a Pinkerton detective, and my denial bears the evidences of truth to substantiate it. But the Pinkerton detectives cannot deny that they murdered my father's half-brother, and shot off the right arm of my grandmother. They cannot deny it because the proofs of the murder are plain. I recently heard my grandmother give the following account of this murder:

"It was long after the war while my boys were hunted everywhere and detectives were coming to my home every little while. One dark midnight while only me and the doctor, and my colored woman and my eight-year-old son, Archie, were alone, a bomb crime crashing through the kitchen window. It was thrown with such force that it smashed the whole sash out and fell on the floor. We ran into the kitchen and there it lay blazing. It was wrapped around with cloth and soaked in oil. We rolled it into the fireplace to keep it from setting the house on fire. Then it exploded. A piece of the shell struck little Archie in the breast, going nearly through him and killing him almost instantly. Another piece tore my right arm off between the wrist and elbow. We rushed out doors but could see no one in the darkness. We found the house had been set afire and was blazing fiercely, but we put it out. Those fiends had intended to kill us all with the bomb and then burn us up. There was a light snow on the ground and the next morning we tracked the cowardly hounds, and it appeared there were eight of them. We found a revolver one of them had dropped, and it was stamped with the Pinkerton name."

My grandmother has yet at her home the half of this iron bomb-shell, and visitors to her home may see it there. It is wrought iron with a shell about one-fourth of an inch thick, and it is eight inches in diameter. The edges are torn and jagged by the force of the explosion that burst it asunder. A photograph of Archie Samuels, who was murdered by the Pinkerton, hangs in a corner in the parlor of my grandmother's home and it shows a bright, sweet faced boy. Beside it on the wall, hanging in a faded frame, is a piece of exceedingly delicate needlework made by grandmother when she was a school girl in a Catholic convent in Kentucky. On the other side of it hangs the picture of a gravestone, and beneath the monument is this inscription:

In Loving Remembrance of My Beloved Son,

Jesse W. James.

Died April 3, 1882.

Aged 34 Years, 6 Months, 28 Days.

Murdered by a Traitor and Coward Whose Name is Not Worthy to Appear Here.

Before my father was killed, my grandmother did not know he was living in St. Joseph. She never knew where he lived at any time after the war, nor anything of his comings and goings. He came often to see her, but would never talk to her about himself. Once, shortly after his marriage, he visited his mother and she asked him where he was living, and he told her:

"Ma, don't ever ask me where my family is."

"Why?" she inquired.

"Because if you knew where we were living, every wind that blew from that direction would make you uneasy."

A year or two ago my grandmother told in my presence and hearing the following to a reporter for the Kansas City Star; and it was printed in that paper:

"A few days ago," said Mrs. Samuels, "a man came here to look around and said to me he believed my boys were after him once.

"No, sir;" I told him, "My boys were never after you. If they had been they'd have got yon. If my boys ever started after a man they always got him.

"My boys were brave. I saw enough of it."

Mrs. Samuels laughed heartily and went on: "I remember one day during the war, Jesse and three more of Quantrell's men rode up here to wash up and change shirts. They told me they were hard chased and while they were washing my colored boy held their horses back of the house and I watched from the front. By and by I saw about forty Federal soldiers going up through the field over there toward old Dan Askew 's house. Dan was a Northern spy. I shouted to Jesse:

"'I see some Federals"

"How many, mother?' asked Jesse.

"About forty."

"Where are they?"

"Going up through the field to old Dan Askew."

"Well, keep your eye on them, mother,' said Jesse, and they went right on washing.

"In a minute I saw them coming down toward our house and I shouted:

"Boys, they're coming to the house."

"Jesse was spluttering with his face down in the water basin and he stopped long enough to say:

"Let 'em come, mother; there are four of us and I guess we can whip forty Federals all right enough."

"I got scared and I ran back to where the boys were washing and begged them to run.

"Do go, Jesse," I said. 'They're crossing the branch and will be right here in half a minute.'

"Jesse just laughed at me and said: 'Don't get rattled, mother. I'm not going away from here with a dirty neck if I have to fight two hundred and forty Federals instead of forty.'

"Well, sir, those four boys did not mount their horses till the soldiers were at the front gate and they heard the latch rattling. Then they sprang into their saddles, and leaped the back fence and rode across the pasture like mad. The Federals galloped around the house, part one way and part the other, and pulled their cavalry pistols, and such shooting and cursing you never heard. Our boys shot back as they ran, and the last I saw of them was a waving line of horses going over the top of the hill. I waited half an hour and then I could stand it no longer. I got on my horse Betsy, and went up over the hill expecting to find the bodies of four boys shot full of holes. About a mile from the house some one hailed me from the brush.

"Where are you going, ma?"'

"It was Jesse, and he and the boys were coming down from the old school house leading their horses and looking for their caps they had lost during the fight. They wouldn't listen to anything I'd say, but rode back to the house with me after they'd found their caps. They washed up again and then rode away.

"Jesse seemed to take delight in getting me scared and playing jokes on me. You know I was always watching out for detectives, and we had plenty of them spying around here. That was long after the war, when Jesse was accused of every bank and train robbery that was done. One day a big man rode up to the gate, hitched his horse and stalked right up to the house and demanded to know where Jesse James was. He said he was a detective and he pulled out a big revolver and threatened to kill him on sight. He took Jesse's gold watch out of his pocket and showed it to me, and said he had killed Jesse and took his watch. I told him I knew he was lying.

He searched the house and barn, bulldozed my colored man and woman, and I followed him around, daring him to harm a hair of anyone around the place. At last he sat down in a chair and laughed until I thought he'd split. He told me he was Dave Poole, a friend of Jesse's, and he handed me' a letter from Jesse, who had told him to pretend he was a detective and give me a scare. Jesse had said to him:

"The old lady may take a shot at you, but if she doesn't hit you, go right in."

"Some of the detectives that came prowling around here had narrow escapes," continued Mrs. Samuels. "You see, they were all cowards; I never saw a detective in all my life who wasn't a coward, and Jesse knew that well enough, too. The detectives used always to come when they thought my boys were away, but two of them missed it once and came very near getting killed. Jesse was here one day when I saw two men coming down the road. We could tell a detective on sight, and we knew they were detectives. They stopped at the gate and hallowed. Jesse stepped just inside the door to the stairway leading to the attic and stood there with his revolvers in his hands. Jesse said:

"Go to the door, mother."

"I opened the door and one of the men said they were cattle buyers, and asked if we had any fat cattle.

"Tell them yes, mother, said Jesse. 'Tell them the cattle are here and for them to come in and get them.'

"The cattle you are looking for are in the house; come in and get them!' I shouted. They talked together awhile in whispers and then went on. I guess that was as near as I ever came to seeing shooting right here in the house.

"But the funniest thing that ever happened was one day when a sheriff—I won't mention his name, because he is living yet—came here alone after Jesse. I had ten harvest hands at work in the field, and Jesse was hiding in the attic. When dinner was ready I brought Jesse down to eat first before the hands came in at noon. Just as he came down stairs there was a knock at the door. Jesse peeped out the window and said it was the sheriff. He drew his revolver and said:

"Open the door, mother."

"I opened it and the sheriff walked in.

"Your gun, please,' Jesse said, as cool as could be, and the sheriff took out his revolver.

"Throw it over on the bed,' ordered Jesse, and he did so.

"Now, sit down and have dinner with us,' commanded Jesse, and the two sat down at the table and chatted like old friends while they ate a hearty meal. After it was over Jesse handed the sheriff his revolver and bid him good-bye. The sheriff never came back. He was always a great friend of my boys after that."

As an instance of the courage displayed by the survivors of Quantrell's guerrilla band, who were persecuted and driven from pillar to post after the war, I will tell here of an adventure of Ciel. Miller, who was hounded by officers because he had been seen in company with my father. Miller had broken his leg in a fall from his horse and was lying at the home of his cousin near Carrollton, Mo. While he was there the sheriff of the county with a posse rode up and surrounded the house. The sheriff dismounted and came to the door and inquired:

"I understand that Ciel. Miller is here?"

"No, he is not here;" answered Miller's cousin, who had answered the knock at the door.

"Yes, he is here. I have the information from a most reliable source. Unless you surrender him at once we will set fire to the house and smoke you all out."

Ciel. Miller was lying on a sofa in the parlor and overheard every word of this conversation. Suddenly he sang out:

"Yes, I am here in the front room with a broken leg and unable to move. Come in sheriff, and I will talk over terms of surrender."

The sheriff knew that Miller's leg had been broken only a few days before. He had no fear of Miller, and he walked boldly in.

"Take a chair and sit down, sheriff, I want to talk to you," said Miller.

The sheriff sat down and Miller said:

"Give me a chance to fight the whole posse, and you can take me, dead or alive."

"No; I will listen to no propositions. You must go along and take your chances at a trial in the court."

"All right; I will go with you if you will give me your promise to protect me from violence at the hands of the posse."

"I will do that. I will be personally responsible for your safety." the sheriff said.

"That is satisfactory. Help me put my overshoe on my good leg and I will go with you."

The sheriff had no reason to suspect that Miller was not sincere. Miller reached under the sofa as if to get his overshoe, but instead of bringing out a shoe he jerked out a revolver and put it to the sheriff's ear. His manner changed instantly from one of politeness to fierceness. He threatened the sheriff with instant death if he did not obey. He took away the sheriff's revolvers and put them in his own pockets. Then he put his left arm around the sheriff's shoulders and leaned upon him for support and with the muzzle of his huge revolver stuck in the sheriff's ear he hobbled on one foot outside the front door. Standing there, in full view of the posse, he called out that if one man advanced a step toward him he would kill the sheriff and then shoot into the posse and kill all he could before he himself was killed. He made the sheriff order the posse to stand back and obey orders. Then the sheriff assisted Miller to the sheriff's horse and helped him mount, the sheriff himself getting up in front of him. Miller ordered the posse to stay where they were, threatening to kill the sheriff if one of them stirred. He rode with the sheriff for three miles and then made him dismount, thanked him, bade him goodbye, and rode away alone in the gathering darkness and escaped.

My father was anxious at all times to surrender to the proper authorities, upon proper guarantees of protection from violence at the hands of his enemies and fair treatment at the hands of the officers of the law. These overtures on his part were spurned. My grandmother and friends of the family went to three different governors of Missouri and begged and pleaded for fair terms upon which he could surrender. My father said to his mother shortly before his death:

"'I would be willing to wear duck clothing all my life if I could only be a free man.'"

But all his pleadings for a fair chance to surrender were spurned. His old enemies were working constantly to prejudice the public and the officers against him. For twelve years every train robbery and every bank robbery in the country was attributed to him. I have looked through the old files of the daily papers published in Kansas City during those years, and it is really ridiculous to see what crimes were charged up to the account of my hunted and outlawed father. This week there would be a bold robbery somewhere in Missouri, and the newspapers in great head lines charge it to "The James Gang Again." The next week there would be a robbery in Texas, and again it would be the "James Gang." To have committed one-fourth of the crimes charged to him my father would have to have been equipped with an air ship or some other means of aerial flight, for no known method of terrestrial transportation could have made it possible for him to rob a bank in West Virginia Monday night and hold up a train in Texas three nights later.

Yet the credulous public believed the most of these stories. And the gangs who were doing these robberies wished the public to so believe, and in most of these robberies the leader always took pains to inform the robbed people that he was Jesse James, or to write a notification to that effect and leave it where it could be found.

The very day upon which my father was killed there was a peculiarly bold and successful hold up and robbery of a train in Texas, and the newspapers over all the country attributed it to Jesse James. If there is anyone who doubts this to be true, he may prove it true by turning back to the files of the daily papers of that date and find the account of this train robbery upon the first page. In most of the newspapers the name "Jesse James" is the first and most prominent headline, and the succeeding headlines tell of how he and his "gang" held up and robbed the train.

And at the very moment this train was robbed my father was lying dead in St. Joseph.

The death of my father did not bring a cessation of train or bank robberies. This nefarious method of robbery went right on and has continued to the present time, and probably will go on, like Tennyson's brook, forever.

The death of my father created one of the greatest sensations that the West had ever known. He was killed April 3, 1882. I have clipped from the Kansas City Journal of April 4, 1882, the news account, head lines and all, of that tragedy, and here reproduce a part of it as a bit of history that will be found deeply interesting to all who have been interested enough in the story this book tells to have read this far into it:

GOODBYE, JESSE!

"I've got him, sure, " was the telegram that came to the city yesterday. It was meaningless to almost everybody, yet it contained news of the greatest importance. Jesse James was the person referred to and as he was a corpse, the sender of the dispatch was confident that he had him, sure.

At 9 o'clock yesterday morning Jesse James was shot dead at St. Joseph, Mo., by Robert Ford, a young man about twenty-one years of age, from Ray County. Ford, being acquainted with the James gang, recently planned the death of Jesse. This plan was concocted in this city, and was, as it has been seen, successfully carried out. His brother Charles was with him at the time of the killing and the wife of Jesse was in the kitchen of the house in which they were living. At his death, Jesse was hanging pictures. He had but a few minutes before being killed, divested himself of his coat and his revolvers. He never spoke a word after falling to the floor. The slayers gave themselves up soon after the killing, and an inquest over the remains was begun.

THE KILLING IN DETAIL
SPECIAL DISPATCH TO THE KANSAS CITY JOURNAL

St. Joseph, Mo., April 3.—Between eight and nine o'clock this morning Jesse James, the Missouri outlaw, before whose record the deeds of Fr. Diavolo, Dick Turpin and Shinterhannes dwindle into insignificance, v/as killed by a boy twenty-one years old, named Robt. Ford at his temporary residence on Thirteenth and Lafayette streets, in this city. In the light of all moral reasoning the shooting was wholly unjustifiable, but the law is vindicated, and the $10,000 reward offered by the state will doubtless go to the man who had the courage to draw a revolver on the notorious outlaw when his back was turned, as in this case. There is little doubt that the killing was the result of a premeditated plan formed by Robert and Charles Ford several months ago. Charles had been an accomplice of Jesse James since the third of last November, and entirely possessed his confidence. Robert Ford, his brother, joined Jesse near Mrs. Samuels (the mother of the James boys), last Friday a week ago, and accompanied Jesse and Charles to this city Sunday, March 23.

Jesse, his wife and two children, removed from Kansas City (where they had lived several months until they feared their whereabouts would be suspected) to this city, arriving here November 8, 1881, coming in a wagon and accompanied by Charles Ford. They rented a house on the corner of Lafayette and Twenty-first streets, where they stayed two months, when they secured the house No. 1381 on Lafayette Street, formerly the property of Councilman Aylesbury, paying fourteen dollars a month for it, and giving the name of Thomas Howard.

The house is a one-story cottage, painted white, with green shutters, and is romantically situated on the brow of a lofty eminence east of the city, commanding a fine view of the principal portion of the city, river and railroads, and adapted by nature for the perilous and desperate calling of Jesse James. Just east of the house is a deep, gulch-like ravine and beyond that a broad expanse of open country backed by a belt of timber.

The house, except from the west side, can be seen for several miles. There is a large yard attached to the cottage, and a stable where Jesse had been keeping two horses, which were found there this morning.

Charles and Robert Ford have been occupying one of the rooms in the rear of the dwelling, and have secretly had an understanding to kill Jesse ever since last fall. Ever since the boys have been with Jesse, they have watched for an opportunity to shoot him, but he was always so heavily armed that it was impossible to draw a weapon without James seeing it. They declared that they had no idea of taking him alive, considering the undertaking suicidal. The opportunity they had long wished for came this morning. Breakfast was over. Charlie Ford and Jesse James had been in the stable currying the horses preparatory to their night ride. On returning to the room where Robert Ford was, Jesse said: "It's an awfully hot day." He pulled off his coat and vest and tossed them on the bed. Then he said, "I guess I'll take off my pistols for fear somebody will see them if I walk in the yard." He unbuckled the belt in which he* carried two 45-calibre revolvers, one a Smith & Wesson and the other a Colt, and laid them on the bed with his coat and vest. He then picked up a dusting brush with the intention of dusting some pictures which hung on the wall. To do this he got on a chair. His back was now turned to the brothers, who silently stepped between Jesse and his revolvers. At a motion from Charlie both drew their guns. Robert was the quickest of the two, and in one motion he had the long weapon to a level with his eye, and with the muzzle not more than four feet from the back of the outlaw's head. Even in that motion, quick as thought, there was something which did not escape the acute ears of the hunted man. He made a motion as if to turn his head to ascertain the cause of that suspicious sound, but too late. A nervous pressure on the trigger, a quick flash, a sharp report and the well directed ball crashed through the outlaw's skull. There was no outcry; just a swaying of the body and it fell heavily backwards upon the carpet of the floor. The shot had been fatal and all the bullets in the chambers of Charlie's revolver still directed at Jesse's head could not more effectually have decided the fate of the greatest bandit and free hooter that ever figured in the pages of a country's history.

The ball had entered the base of the skull and made its way out through the forehead, over the left eye. It had been fired out of a Colt's 45 improved pattern, silver mounted and pearl handled pistol presented by the dead man to his slayer only a few days ago.

Mrs. James was in the kitchen when the shooting was done, separated from the room in which the bloody tragedy occurred by the dining room. She heard the shot, and dropping her household duties ran into the front room. She saw her husband lying extended his back, his slayers, each holding his revolver in his hand, making for the fence in the rear of the house. Robert had reached the enclosure and was in the act of scaling it when she stepped to the door and called to him: "Robert, you have done this, come back." Robert answered: "I swear to God I didn't." They then returned to where she stood. Mrs. James ran to the side of her husband and lifted up his head. Life was not yet extinct and when she asked him if he was hurt, it seemed to her that he wanted to say something, but could not. She tried to wash away the blood that was coursing over his face from the hole in his forehead, but it seemed to her that the blood would come faster than she could wipe it away, and in her hands Jesse James died.

Charlie Ford explained to Mrs. James that "a pistol had accidentally gone of it." "Yes," said Mrs. James, "I guess it went off on purpose" Meanwhile Charlie had gone back in the house and brought out two hats, and the two boys left the house. They went to the telegraph office, sent a message to Sheriff Timberlake, of Clay County; to Police Commissioner Craig, of Kansas City; to Governor Crittenden, and other officers, and then surrendered themselves to Marshal Craig.

When the Ford boys appeared at the police station, they were told by an officer that Marshall Craig and a posse of officers had gone in the direction of the James residence and they started after them and surrendered themselves. They accompanied the officers to the house and returned in custody of the police to the marshal's headquarters, where they were furnished with dinner, and about 3 p. m. were removed to the old circuit court room, where the inquest was held in the presence of an immense crowd. Mrs. James accompanied the officers to the house, having previously left her two children, aged seven and three years, a boy and a girl, at the house of a Mrs. Terrel, who had known the James' under their assumed name of Howard ever since they had occupied the adjoining house. She was strongly affected by the tragedy, and the heart-rending moans and expressions of grief were sorrowful evidence of the love she bore for the dead desperado.

The report of the killing of the notorious outlaw spread like wildfire throughout the city, and as usual the report assumed every variety of form and color. Very few accredited the news, however, and simply laughed at the idea that Jesse James was really the dead man.

Nevertheless the excitement ran high, and when one confirming point succeeded the other, crowds of hundreds gathered at the undertaking establishment where lay the body. At the city hall, at the court house, and in fact on every street corner, the almost incredible news constituted the sole topic of conversation, to the exclusion of the barely less engrossing topic of the coming election.

Coroner Heddens was notified, and Undertaker Sidenfaden instructed to remove the body to his establishment. This was about 10 o'clock. A large crowd accompanied the coroner to the undertaker's, but only the wife and the reporters were admitted. The body lay in a remote room of the building. It had been taken out of the casket and placed upon a table. The features appeared natural, but were disfigured by the bloody hole over the left eye. The body was neatly and cleanly dressed; in fact, nothing in the appearance of the remains indicated the desperate career of the man or the many bloody scenes of which he had been the hero. The large, cavernous eyes were closed as in a calm slumber. Only the lower part of the face, the square cheek bones, the stout, prominent chin covered with a soft, sandy beard, and the thin, firmly closed lips, in a measure betrayed the determined will and iron courage of the dead man. A further inspection of the body revealed two large bullet wounds on the right side of the breast, within three inches of the nipple, a bullet wound in the leg and the absence of the tip of the middle finger of the left hand.

THE NEWS IN KANSAS CITY

The news of the killing of the famous outlaw created such an excitement on the streets of Kansas City as had not existed since the assassination of President Garfield. Everybody was talking of it yesterday afternoon, and it was frequently heard that it was "decidedly too thin." People would not believe it, and it is probable that when the patrons of the Journal read the account of it this morning that many of them will be unable to realize that the famous bandit, whose name is better known in Missouri than that of any statesman in America, has ended his eventful career. Groups gathered on the street corners to discuss the matter, and even the all absorbing question of city politics was abandoned to ask "who killed him?" "when did it happen?" etc. The most ignorant as well as the wisest of the citizens were interested in the matter, and every representative of the press, as well as the members of the police force, were besieged with anxious inquiries. Occasionally a man is seen who denounces the deed as cowardly, and the wish was heard to be expressed that the man who did the killing might hang. At the station there was a crowd all the afternoon anxious to hear the very latest news. Mayor Frank and a crowd of the clerks and city officials were engaged in an animated discussion of the affair. Said the mayor: "I fully believe that he is dead this time."

The Kansas City Times on this day printed the following description of Jesse James;

Jesse James was about 5 feet 11 inches in height, of a rather solid, firm and compact build, yet rather of the slender type. His hair was black, not overly long; blue eyes, well shaded with dark lashes, and the entire lower portion of his face was covered by a full growth of dark brown or sun browned whiskers, which are not long and shaggy, but are trimmed and bear evidence of careful attention. His complexion was fair, and he was not sunburn to any considerable extent, as the reader is generally led to suppose. He was neatly clad in a business suit of cassimere, of dark brown substance, which fit him very neatly. He wore a shirt of spotless whiteness, with collar and cravat, and looked more the picture of a staid and substantial business man than the outlaw and desperado that he was.

The widow of Jesse James was a neat and rather prepossessing lady, and bears the stamp of having been well brought up and surrounded by influences of a better and of a holier character than the reader would at first suppose. She is rather slender, fair of face, light hair, blue eyes, with high forehead and marks of intelligence very strikingly apparent. The two children, a little boy and girl, were neat and intelligent, and seemed to grieve much over the deed which had in one short moment deprived them of a father ^s love and protection.

The Kansas City Times of April 7, 1882, published the following account of the funeral of Jesse James:

Special to the Kansas City Times.

Kearney, April 6.—Yesterday was a holiday at Kearney, near which is the home of Mrs. Samuels, mother of the noted Jesse James. Kearney is a town of between four hundred and five hundred inhabitants, situated on the Hannibal and St. Joe railway, twenty-four miles from Kansas City. At an early hour from all directions came people on the trains, on horseback and in vehicles, anxious to gaze upon the remains of the dead bandit. The metallic casket containing the body was taken to the Kearney house upon its arrival at 2:45 a. m. It was placed upon chairs in the office, and during the forenoon and a portion of the afternoon was surrounded by friends, relatives and strangers anxiously peering into the pallid features. No one who claimed to know him in life doubted that the remains were those of Jesse James. Photographs of the deceased in possession of the Times correspondent were compared with the corpse, and admitted by many of his friends to be genuine. No ill will was engendered or if any existed those possessing it were careful not to let their passions get the better of them. It seemed to be understood by everyone that the solemnity of the occasion demanded that everything be done decently and in order.

THE FUNERAL PROCESSION

Long before noon the town was full of people. The funeral procession started for the Baptist church, in which Jesse was converted in 1866. The edifice was filled, and for many there was standing room only. The pall bearers were J. D. Ford, Deputy Marshal J. T. Reed, Charles Scott, James Henderson and William Bond. There was another, a sixth pall bearer, a rather mysterious character, whom none of the other five seemed to know. He seemed to have charge of the cortege and directed the movements but neither his fellow pall bearers nor the bystanders knew who he was. He was a stout and well preserved man, of perhaps forty years, and seemed to understand what he was about, but no one could say who he was or where he came from.

The relatives, consisting of Mrs. Samuels, Mrs. James and two children, Mr. and Mrs. Luther W. James, Mrs. Hall and Mrs. Mimms, were seated beside the coffin, placed in front of the altar. The services were opened by singing the hymn, "What a Friend We Have in Jesus." Rev. R. H. Jones, of Lathrop, read a passage of scripture from Job, commencing, "Man born of woman is of few days and full of trouble." Also the fourth and fifth verses of the 39th Psalm, beginning, "Lord, make me to know mine end." He offered up a touching and pathetic prayer for the grief stricken mother, wife and children asked the Lord to make their bereavement a blessing to them, by leading them to a true knowledge of himself.

THE FUNERAL SERMON

Rev. J. M. P. Martin, pastor of the church, as an introduction to his discourse said: We all understand that we cannot change the state of the dead. Again, it would be useless for me to bring any new information before this congregation respecting the life and character of the deceased.

The text which I have chosen to-day is the 24th chapter of Matthew, 44th verse: "Therefore be ye ready, for in such an hour as ye think not the Son of Man Cometh.' First, I wish to call special attention to the certainty of the coming of Christ to each of us. There is a certainty of a grave before each of us. We cannot jump over it or pass it by. God's word is written on His tablets for our instruction and guidance. It takes it for granted that there is a certainty of death. It is constantly warning us of this solemn fact. We talk of death to others, and dwell upon its terrors and are stricken down with grief when it lays its hand upon those we love, but seem unwilling to regard its certainty to ourselves. The truth I wish you to take home with you today is that Christ is sure to come to each of us. In the second place, Christ is sure to come at such an hour as we think not. He comes like a thief in the night. As the thief comes when we are least expecting it, so Christ comes. Whatever the past has been, we all have our idle dreams of the future. We all in our imagination have fancy pictures, and are apt to forget the evils that are likely to befall us. If we could at all learn a lesson from the past, we would not expect the future as our fancy paints it. Though we are assured that others shall die and not live, we feel for ourselves we shall live and not die. Shall we not set about for a future which is as real as life is real? Our expectation then of the lengthening out of our lives will not keep away the coming of the Son of Man. Let us remember that He comes as a thief in the night, and not delay our preparations. But it seems idle to try to get men to make preparation for what seems imaginary.

We will not entertain the fact as it is. It is necessary for us to prepare to meet our God. If men are so careful to prepare for things that pertain to this life, how much more important is it to prepare for things that pertain to the life to come? If we accept Christ our account will be acceptable to our Lord. How would we feel if God should come and we should be compelled to stand before Him unprepared? As I said before, we cannot change the past life or condition of the dead. I ask you to take your eyes off from that coffin; I ask you to take your eyes off from the open grave and look higher. Let us not forget our duties and responsibilities in life. A true prophet is not without honor saves in his own land, and those who point the way to righteousness are often unheeded. Notwithstanding the many unheeded warnings, God is constantly reminding us and calling us to Him. At the same time that He points us to the grave and tells us to look into it. He says to us it is not all of death to die, not all of life to live. But we need not die spiritually. All we need do is to look and live. Yet we turn away, and turn away until our hearts become hard as stone. He asks us to turn to Him and promises us everlasting life. What more could he say? Let us see that we make ready and stand ready when He calls to us.

Before the coffin is taken from the house, I have been asked to make one or two requests. As John Samuels is very low on account of the shock caused by the death of his brother, and as the grave is very near the house, Mrs. Samuels asks that those who are here will not go out to the house. It is feared that the excitement of seeing so many persons present will injure him. It is therefore requested that none but the friends and relatives go to the grave.

My father was buried in a corner of the beautiful yard that surrounds my grandmother's home, the house in which he was born. The grave is beneath a giant coffee bean tree, and it is covered by flowers that are tended by his mother. A monument of white marble marks the grave.

CHAPTER IX. JESSE JAMES, JR.

I come now to where I must speak of myself and the family left when my father was killed. Not long after his death, my mother and her two children moved to Kansas City to live and to earn a living. I was eleven years old when I answered an advertisement of a "Boy wanted," and it led me to the office of Thomas T. Crittenden, Jr., son of the T. T. Crittenden who was governor of Missouri when my father was killed. T. T. Crittenden, Jr., was in the real estate business, and it was to his office that I unwittingly went in reply to the advertisement and applied for work. He was greatly surprised, I have learned since, when I, together with other boys who were applicants for the place, wrote my name upon a sheet of paper to give him a sample of my handwriting. He employed me in preference to any other boy who was there, and I found in him the best and truest friend that I have ever known. He sold to my mother a lot of ground in Kansas City and loaned us the money to build a modest house upon it, taking my notes for the amount and assuring us that the notes should never go out of his hands, and that we should have our own time in which to pay them off. He kept his word. I remained with him as his office boy for one year. I went to school until I was fifteen years of age. Then I went to work in the Armor packing plant, and remained there six and one-half years, when I opened a cigar stand in the county court house.

In all those years that I was working for wages I was paying a part of my earnings each month taking up the mortgage on our home. The balance of my wages went to help support my mother and sister and to keep my sister at school. She graduated from the High School in the class of '98.

The most gratifying thing to me in all my life was when I was under arrest on a false charge of train robbery and men whom I had worked for, and men of well known integrity and honor in the community, who had lived near me and watched me grow up, took the witness stand voluntarily and testified under oath that they knew no young man in the city whose character was better than mine or whom they would trust farther. Since I was old enough to know anything I had striven industriously to build up and establish just that kind of a character and reputation, and when a set of unscrupulous detectives sought by false charges to tear down in a day what I had spent the few years of my life in building up, it was peculiarly satisfying to me to see that I was trusted and believed in by men whose regard I would rather have than the good will of all the detectives who ever lived and lied.

I come now to an account of that conspiracy which was intended to be my utter ruin, and the ruin of my mother and sister as well. This conspiracy, hatched in the brains of detectives, was intended by ruining me and mine to pay off old scores that the detective fraternity had against the James family for years past.

CHAPTER X.THE LEEDS HOLD UP

What is known in the criminal annals of Jackson County, Missouri, as "The Leeds Hold-up" occurred the night of September 23, 1898, on the Missouri Pacific road near Leeds, Mo., eight miles south of Kansas City. In order to understand the events that followed this hold-up, resulting at last in my arrest and trial for the crime, it is best to give here the account of the robbery as it was published the next day in the Kansas City Star. That account, written by one of the most graphic writers on that great newspaper, follows:

The dull explosion that was heard throughout the southeastern part of the city last night was the work of train robbers. It was not much after ten o'clock when the robbers dynamited the express car of a southbound Missouri Pacific train a few miles beyond Leeds and eight miles from Kansas City. That they did not blow off their own clothing was a wonder, for the car was razed, the great iron safe was shattered, and, for a distance of two miles, waybills and papers and fragments of baggage were scattered along the track. The party of masked bandits, thinking they had cut the telegraph wires to Kansas City, used no stint in the application of dynamite. They left a card with the express messenger stating that the supply of quails was good.

A MERRY LITTLE TRAIN ROBBER JOKE

Chief Hayes has in his possession the only tangible clue of the man who did the work. It is a card handed to Express Messenger E. N. Hills by one of the robbers after they had finished. On one side is printed: "Vote for Robert W. Green, Republican nominee for county collector of Jackson County." On the reverse side this is printed with a dull lead pencil:

We, the masked knights of the road, robbed the M. P. train at the Belt Line junction tonight. The supply of quails was good. "With much love we remain, John Kennedy, Bill Ryan, Bill Anderson, Sam Brown, Jim Redmond.

Whoever the robbers are, one of them, the author of the printed card, evidently has a smattering of Latin, as the last line on the card is "we are excerpter to." This is undoubtedly intended for ex co7ispectu, meaning "out of sight." So the last words would read, "we are out of sight."

The Pacific Express company declares it lost nothing except smashed express matter. Last night officials of the company said that everything of value in the safe had been blown to pieces.

The whole affair took only a few minutes. At 9:40 o'clock the Wichita-Little Rock express stopped at the Pittsburgh & Gulf junction, fewer than eight miles south of Kansas City, and in thirty minutes the sound of the explosion was heard in the city.

Word of the hold-up reached police headquarters between 10:30 and 11:00o'clock. It was more than an hour past midnight when a special train bearing railroad and express officials, and police officers, started for the scene.

After an hour of rushing and jerking through the inky darkness, the lights of a train were made out. Standing just across a trestle at what is most commonly known as "P. & G. Junction," was the southbound Little Rock and Wichita express. It swarmed with passengers. They were loud in their praises of the dispatch and nerve of the robbers. It was all over before they knew anything about it. Leaning out of the mail car, which had the front of the train, was John Nelson, the mail clerk.

"How did it happen?" "Hanged if I know," he explained. "I heard a shot and looked out, and then I stayed inside my car."

"Where's the engine?"

"Took it west of Swope Park and blew it up."

THE OPERATOR S STORY

Beside the trestle and the train, the only other things to be made out in the darkness were the lights of a little shanty, a hundred yards away. Therein a blonde mustached man labored patiently with a battered telegraph apparatus.

"The tall man smashed it," he explained, "while the short man covered me with a Winchester!"

Between his efforts to make 'the instrument work the operator added that the place was "P. & G, Junction" sometimes called Brush Creek junction and Belt Line junction, where the Kansas City, Pittsburg & Gulf crosses the southbound Missouri Pacific, between Leeds and Dodson. He was D. M. Hisey, the Pittsburg & Gulf railway operator.

"It was just before the Missouri Pacific No. 5 was due," he said, "that they came in. By they I mean the tall man and the short man. The short man had a black mask over his face. He shoved a "Winchester into my stomach and ordered me to throw up my hands. The tall man had a cloth tied over his face. The mask on the short man slipped down, and I saw his nose and the upper part of his face. He had a big red nose.

"The tall man had a revolver and a pair of wire pliers. He tried to cut the wires and smashed at the switchboard with his revolver when he was unable to cut the cables."

To appreciate this scene it should be understood that the little telegraph room is just big enough to contain three men and a gun.

"Just then the train crossed the trestle, and as it always does, stopped," continued Hisey. "The short man shoved me along at the muzzle of the Winchester, down the track to the train. I noticed that the mouthpiece of his mask was down over his chin. Around the engine were several men with black masks. They had the engineer and fireman down from the engine. They swore horribly. I think I saw seven of them. There was a shot. I was ordered, along with the engineer, to uncouple the engine and express car. We complied! Did we comply quickly? You bet we did! Then they said to us:

"Get on the train and stay on there, or we'll kill you!'

"Then they whistled for a flagman and went off with the engine. About twenty minutes afterward we heard a tremendous explosion. The express messenger came running back and said the express car had been blown up. I began fixing my instruments and sent a message to Kansas City. The big fellow who tried to cut off telegraphic communication was a lobster and didn't know how to do it."

The engine of the relief train pushed the robbed and engineless express car ahead, for it was impossible to pass it. It held the track. It was a slow, noisy procession. About one-half mile further on the caravan of coaches came upon a strange scene.

WRECKAGE ALONG THE TRACK

Looming up in the flare of torches were two Kansas City policemen, Sergeant Caskey and Officer Harry Adams, who had driven out in a buggy and beaten the train. The conductor of the ill-fated train, Hans Carr, several deputy marshals, and a number of negroes with guns, were delving in a mass of debris by the track side in the weird torchlight. Broken trunks, women's finery, fragments of car roofs, a bicycle, men's underclothing, blackened valises, and a pulpy mass of a hundred different things were piled and scattered in the ditch along the left hand side of the track. The telegraph wires were festooned with wreckage. Here the express car had been blown up, but where was the car?

'We're from the coal camp,' said the armed negroes. "We heard the explosion and came over to find out about it."

The railway and express officials fell to heaving the fragments of baggage and express matter into the empty baggage car brought with the relief train. They found half of a 32-caliber revolver twisted as if given a wrench when heated red hot. A little lantern was found in the grass, intact, not a crack in its dainty glass. A section man picked up a sack of tobacco, dry and sweet. Working hardest of all was E. N. Hills, the express messenger. He had lost his hat, and a child's soldier cap, picked up in the wreckage, hung over a bump on his head where a robber struck him with the butt of a revolver. The express officials had a long talk with him before he talked of his experience. Then he denied being given a card with the message from Kennedy and Redmond, saying: "We are the quail hunters."

THE MESSENGER'S EXPERIENCE

"I was working away," said Hills, a smooth faced, nervous young man, "when I felt that my car was starting without the rest of the train. I looked out and saw some figures of men. I realized it was a hold-up and ducked in. Then they came to the side door and beat on it with their guns.

"Let us in or we'll blow you up!' they said."

"Where was your riot gun?" asked Mr. Moore.

"I got a shell jammed in it," explained Hills.

"And you let them in?"

"To be plain about it," replied Hills to his chief, "I didn't feel justified in losing my life. I had no chance to put up a fight. I opened the door and three got in. They were masked and carried sacks over their arms. One man got the drop on me.

They cursed me and asked how much money there was in the safe. I lied to them good and plenty. "They didn't ask me for the combination of the through safe, because they knew I didn't have it had a good deal of talk. The mask of the man with the Winchester slipped and I tried to get a good look at him. Quick as a flash he hit me on the head with the butt of his revolver.

"Meanwhile we were moving away. They put seven sticks of dynamite on top of the safe, set the small portable safe the local safe which I showed them was empty, on top of the dynamite. The car stopped and they set a fuse. I saw a match struck. They jumped out leaving me in the car.

"You stay and see how it goes!' they told me.

"It was an awful moment. I begged for my life. I pleaded with them and they let me jump down. We all moved up on the other side of the engine. It seemed an age and there was no explosion. They explained that the fuse had gone out. I was afraid they would order me to go inside to investigate. Instead they told me to uncouple the car from the engine. Just as I was doing it there was a flash and roar. It seemed to me I was within a foot of it! I fell down.

"Git!' somebody said, and I got down the track!"

THE WRECKED CAR AFIRE

The caravan went on through the darkness. It was now three o'clock in the morning. Somebody said that men had been seen driving rapidly through the darkness toward Kansas City in a buggy, just after the robbery. Employees of the Diamond Brick works asserted they heard two explosions following the first great explosion. At a point which the railway men said was about three and one-half miles beyond the junction, burned a fitful, sullen fire. It was the wrecked express car and the killed engine.

What a wreck it was! The car was literally razed to the flat car. Twisted irons and a flat, tangled mass of baggage, express matter and timbers, burned like a gigantic spent fire cracker or a huge bit of "punk." On the left side of the wreck, on the ground, lay the great iron safe. Its top was stove in and it was shattered as if riddled by a thirteen inch shell. The crowds pulled out lumps of the fire proof cement lining as mementoes.

City police, deputy marshals, sections hands, railway officials, passengers in dishabille from the sleeper, tall, thin strangers who came out of the darkness, gathered about the shattered safe helplessly.

FAMILIAR WITH RAILROADING

Charles Slocum, the engineer, and G. L. Weston, the fireman, said that they found the engine without water in the boilers and the crown sheet in danger of blowing out. They had drawn the fire to save the engine. They did not think the robbers were railroad men.

"Even farmers can throw a throttle nowadays," they said.

Nevertheless, it was strange that the robber engineer blew five blasts for a flagman as he pulled out with the engine, notifying the train crew to send back a flagman, if he was a railroad ignoramus.

When the train crew came up to the wreck they found it burning fiercely, and pulled off a good deal of debris to stop the fire. The big safe hung on one side by its iron stanchions, and the train crew and section men pushed it off. Such a joker dynamite is! The fierce shock that razed a staunch car did not harm its trucks, and it was brought to Kansas City at daylight this morning. The small, portable safe was not in sight anywhere. It seemed to have been blown into inky space. Yet a barrel—a mere flimsy barrel—from which stuck wisps of straw, stood unharmed and untouched in a corner wherefrom the walls had been ripped to the floor I Several trunks were uninjured, while the contents of others made a soft, pulpy carpet of the floor of the wrecked car.

Scattered over the whole face of the scene were these cards:

ALBERT HAMILTON DENTON

AND

ALICE EMILY YOUNG,

Married, Tuesday, September 27, 1898,

Arkansas City, Kas

"If there was anything in that safe," said Superintendent Moore of the Pacific express, "it was blown into smithereens! The robbers did not get a cent!"

Two days after this robbery Governor Stephens offered three hundred dollars reward, and the County Court offered five hundred dollars reward, for the capture and conviction of any one of the robbers, making eight hundred dollars reward in all, a prize well worth working for by detectives.

About this time there came upon the scene Thomas Furlong, of the Furlong Secret Service Agency, and Del Harbaugh, his chief assistant. Furlong was the detective of the Missouri Pacific railroad. Harbaugh was a man who had been a hack driver, and all around tough and "disreputable," for years in Lawrence, Kas., until he had been picked up by Furlong and given a commission as a private detective. Furlong turned over to Harbaugh the job of running to earth the robbers, and gaining thereby the reward, and whatever fame and glory would come from the achievement of such a clever detective feat.

Harbaugh made his headquarters at the Savoy hotel. The following newspaper account of his doings, printed in the Kansas City Star, September 30, shows how his work was looked upon by a newspaper reporter:

Headquarters for operations against the robbers have been transferred to the Savoy hotel, where Thomas Furlong, Del Harbaugh and other railroad detectives are staying. The movements of these men are exceedingly mysterious. Bell boys are kept on the jump delivering telegrams to the sleuths. The doors to their private apartments are locked and the keyholes stuffed with paper. There isn't a bell boy in the hotel who has read a line of "Old Cap Collier" or "Young Sleuth" for a week. Fiction has been discarded to watch the movements of real live detectives working on real live clues.

UP STAIRS AND DOWN AGAIN

Chief Hayes and Marshal Chiles pay hourly visits to the big sleuths at the hotel. They go up and down stairs silently and talk in whispers. The mystery of it all is enough to drive bell boys and chambermaids to distraction.

Last night Chief Hayes paced the length of the hotel office mopping the sweat from his face. Harbaugh and Furlong tip-toed down stairs and then the trio tip-toed up stairs. They were followed by John DeLong, the Missouri Pacific detective, who long ago acquired the sobriquet of "Gum Shoes." Later J. H. Schumacher, manager of the Pinkerton agency, came along and found his way on tip -toes to Furlong's room. There they deliberated while a row of bell-boys stood in the hall expecting every minute to hear shots, shouts, screams and a wild denouement of the daring robbery. Even Sam Campbell, the hotel clerk, has grown nervous watching the mysterious actions of his guests.

After last night's conference Furlong took a late train out of town. Harbaugh had been out of town during the night before.

At the county marshal's office this morning telegrams came and went thick and fast. Mr. Chiles said he had nothing to give out, but that the robbers would be under arrest very soon. Chief Hayes said the same thing. Detectives who have not been "let in" on the case declared that this talk was all without foundation and was a ruse to gain time. They say the trail is getting cold. However, the story comes from sources of reliability that one suspect is actually in the hands of the officers.

A search of the hotels failed to find the prisoner, but there are thousands of places where the police could hide a prisoner and keep him safe from reporters. The man under arrest is said to be a former railway employee. Detectives hint that the sweating process applied to the prisoner has been fruitful. They promise that other arrests are to follow quickly.

THE THEORIES NOW

The theory of the detectives is that two of the robbers did not come to the city after the robbery; that they were countrymen and that they live not far from the place where the train was robbed. The railroad detectives say the Leeds robbery was the best planned of its kind that was ever committed in Missouri. Every detail was so carefully carried out as to leave no doubt that old hands did the work.

The story that the thieves got only twenty-nine dollars for their work is hooted at as absurd. The Pinkertons insisted upon knowing exactly how much money was taken before they went to work on the case. It goes out now that the robbers got at least twenty-five thousand dollars.

A telegram was received at police headquarters this morning from Constable Withers of Mayview, Mo., saying that he had arrested two suspicious looking men who he thought might be train robbers. The men carried Winchester rifles and large caliber self-acting revolvers, and displayed plenty of money. Chief Hayes will send two detectives to Mayview tonight to bring the men to Kansas City.

SMITH'S TALE

J. D. Smith, a man whom no one seems to know, came to Kansas City last night with

Detective De Long ("Gum Shoes") of the Missouri Pacific railway secret service. Mr. Smith has harrowing and hair splitting details to tell of how he overheard the planning of the recent hold-up in a box car at Ottawa, Kas., by three men whom he can positively identify. The story, coming as it does from a man in close touch with Detective DeLong, who is noted for being able to supply necessary details when no one else can furnish them, is given little attention by those who are given to taking the train robbery seriously.

Mr. Smith is a man of medium height, dark complexion and shrewd little eyes. He has a small, dashing mustache and a little wisp of hair on his under lip. He hinted his story to a reporter for The Star this morning in an apparently very reluctant manner, with promises of the details tomorrow morning. In answer to vigorous questioning he said about the following:

"It was in a box car at Ottawa, Kas., on the Tuesday night before the hold-up. Shortly after midnight three men got in the car and planned the hold-up. I saw them when they left the car at daylight, and can positively identify them. Later in the morning I saw them on the streets of Ottawa, and at noon I ate dinner at some restaurant with one of them. I learned from the conversation in the box car that one of the men is a bandit and outlaw from the Indian Territory.

HE BIEPT HIS SECRET

"I went to Omaha to see the exposition, and while in a barber shop I read in a paper of the holdup. I kept the secret until I was on my way home, and somewhere between Omaha and Pattonsburg I told the Missouri Pacific conductor what I knew. I was on my way home to Halstead, Kas. The conductor telegraphed for Mr. DeLong, and he met me at Hiawatha, Kas., and brought me here."

"Have you identified the man who is under arrest?" he was asked.

"I cannot talk today. Wait until tomorrow."

"How do you identify the men you heard in the box car."

"I can't talk today."

"What is your business?" Mr. Smith was asked.

"I am a house painter by trade."

Chief Hayes was asked what he thought of Smith's story.

"What Smith? Who is Smith?" he answered.

"The man who was brought here by Detective DeLong," he was told.

"Oh," said the chief, with a look and a smile that meant worlds, "Oh, rats."

September 27, William W. Lowe, a railroad switchman, was arrested by the detectives with great secrecy and hidden away at the police station in Westport, and kept there for weeks, until he finally made what he purported to be a full and complete confession of his part and the part of others in the Leeds hold-up. This confession was as follows:

"The following is my true statement of the train robbery on the Missouri Pacific railway at Belt junction on September 23, 1898, at or about the hour of ten p.m.

:

"The said robbery was planned and arranged for September 21, 1898, but was postponed on account of rain until Friday night, September 23, 1898. The robbery was planned by myself, Andy Ryan and Jesse James, Jr. We three did not want to go alone, so Jesse James, jr., said he had some friends, who he called Charlie and the old man, and also a large man by the name of Evans.

On the night of September 23, I left my home about 6:50 p. m., and took a Summit street car, and rode to the end of the Troost avenue line, from where I went to Thirty-fourth and Tracy avenue and met Jesse James, jr., and he told me that there was a buggy hitched in front of the two little brick houses south of his place, unoccupied. I went there and got the buggy. I drove around on Troost avenue and then back on Thirty-fifth street by a little clump of three or four small trees, and there I met another rig with a dark horse. They drove by me and stopped, and this man they called Charlie got out and came over to me and asked me where was the "Kid." The old man was fixing something on the right shaft of the buggy that he was afraid would let go.

"There were four of us then that showed up—the big man would not get there before 8 p. m. Jesse James, jr., brought the sack which contained the costumes and guns. The costumes consisted of overalls, old hats, jackets and masks. This big man came, that made five, and then came Andy Ryan, which made up the party of six men.

Jesse James, jr., Andy Ryan and myself got in the first buggy; Charlie and the old man and the big man got in the other buggy. Then we all drove east on Thirty-fifth street till we came to the rock road (Indiana avenue is known as the rock road), went south on the rock road to a point close to Brush creek, took the first road east after crossing Brush creek, for some distance, then turned into an old field, turned the buggies around facing the south and dressed, putting on masks and disguises.

"I had on a pair of blue overalls, a check jacket, white hat and black mask; I had on a canvas belt with a big brass buckle, on one side of the buckle were three cartridge holders cut off. I cut them off myself. I had two revolvers stuck in the belt. I had in the hip pocket of my pants a 38-caliber revolver belonging to Henry Simms. I also had a 44-caliber revolver, which I carried in my hand; belongs to Dick Spaw.

THE OLD MAN UNARMED

"When we were dressed it was arranged for the old man to hold the horses. He said he had no gun. I gave him a little Colt's revolver, 38-caliber, that shoots a rim fire cartridge; it was an old style powder and ball, with a cartridge cylinder. To load it you had to knock a pin out and take the cylinder off. The sight was knocked off the end of the barrel. This gun was not returned to me.

"We five went through the weeds to the railroad track, cat-a-corner, and cut a wire fence; went north on the Missouri Pacific track opposite the telegraph office.

"Andy Ryan and Jesse James, jr., went over to the telegraph office and took charge of the operator and destroyed all communication with Kansas City.

"Myself, Charlie and the big man went down to capture the train. As the train came to a stop, with the air applied, and before the air was released, I shut off the cock at the forward end of the baggage car, holding the air set so he could not release it from the engine. I was then standing on the left side of the train going south.

"I crossed over the platform of the baggage car to the right hand side and got up to the engine, and drove the engineer and fireman down to the big man. Charlie searched them to see if they had any guns.

"I took possession of the cab and blew the whistle five times, a signal for the flagman to protect rear end of train.

Andy Ryan and Jesse James, jr., then came up with the operator. Charlie was on the engine with me; the big man, engineer and fireman and operator went and cut the baggage car loose from the train. I started the engine and when the cars were separated about ten feet, the air set; I got down on the cab and shut off the cock at back end of the tank and 'bled' the car; that released the brake on the car.

"I then boarded the engine and pulled out. We stopped at the whistling post for wagon crossing. I stayed on the engine and filled the toiler with water. I got down off the engine and joined the party with the express messenger on the 'Frisco' track.

"I put a gun to the messenger's head and told him, 'God damn you, you got a key to that little safe and I want it.' He said he had given it to them, meaning the members of the party who robbed the train.

"This messenger was taking a good look at one of the men with his mask off ; his attention was directed to it and he made the messenger about face.

"The dynamite did not go off. I and the big man got into the car; there are two doors in the car—double doors. The safe was north of the door on the east side of the car. Dynamite was laid on top of the safe. The little safe was placed on top of the dynamite. I took my pocket knife and split the fuse. Then I struck a match and lit it, jumped out of the car, and then we thought it was not going to go again, so I got on the engine.

"They ordered the express messenger to cut the engine off, and then the dynamite went off and blow the safe. We went back to the car and found it all dark and full of smoke.

"There was d lot of silver dollars in a pine box. After the explosion it was scattered all over the floor. What was got out of the safe was put in a sack and carried away by the big man.

"I supposed the engine was cut off from the car. I pulled up to the road crossing and there we burned up in the fire box of the engine all the costumes, masks, etc., except my overalls and belt. We then went to our buggies and left in the same order we went out in.

"Between the hold-up and Leeds I threw away my overalls and belt. We came on the rock road to Thirty-fifth street, turned west and went to Tracy avenue. There Jesse James, jr., got out and left the shotgun and revolvers in the weeds. My 44 was left there also—this is the gun that belongs to Dick Spaw. Jesse said he. would leave it in the weeds or put it in the cellar of one of the vacant houses.

"The shotgun Jesse had was a double barrel, breech loader, with hammers, and the case found in the buggy belonged to this gun. It was a heavy gun.

"'We all got back in the buggy and drove to one block of the end of the Holmes street line, where Ryan got out. Jesse and I drove to the corner of block east of stable, where I got out and took the laprobe and rubbed the sweat off the horse.

"I went through a vacant lot cat-a-corner. About midway of the block I threw away a handful of 38-caliber cartridges. I came out of the vacant block at the north-west corner through a gate which I found open, boarded a Holmes street car, got on front end on right side of car. Sat on the seat facing east. Andy Ryan was on the car, sitting beside me. We got off the car at Fourteenth street and Grand avenue and went to Fourteenth and Main, and got a glass of beer. We then went up Fourteenth street to Broadway and parted, Ryan going west on Fourteenth and I south on Broadway to Sixteenth and thence west on Sixteenth to my home, arriving at home at 11 :15 p. m.

"The old man I refer to is about my height; weight about 150 pounds. From conversation I inferred that this old man is a relative of Polk's, and lives with Polk or near him. The big man known to me as Evans is described as follows: About six feet tall, weight 175 to 190 pounds, said to have come from Texas, and is a friend of Polk's. I understand he is a friend of Seth Lowe, in Crackerneck.

The inducements that were offered to Lowe to make this confession will be shown in the following chapter, as it was proven at my trial. There is no doubt in the minds of anyone who heard the trial that Lowe was really in the hold-up. He was promised immunity if he would connect me with the robbery, and this promise was kept, because, immediately after my honorable acquittal by a fair and intelligent jury of twelve of the best citizens of the county, the indictment against Lowe was dismissed, and this self-confessed train robber walked out of the court room a free man. The cases against all of the other alleged train robbers were also dismissed and they were discharged from custody. This is positive proof, to me at least, that the detectives were after me alone, and failing to convict me, did not wish that justice be done, and did not seem to care whether train robbers ran at large in the community or not.

I was arrested October 11, 1898, charged with being the leader of a gang of robbers who held up the train at Leeds. The arrest created a great sensation, of course. I quote again from the Kansas City Star, my motive in giving newspaper accounts of this matter being that the public cannot then accuse me of distorting the facts to favor myself, and certainly no one who read the accounts of this affair in the Star would ever suspect that paper of being biased in my favor. The Star said of my arrest:

"The arrest of young Jesse James aroused and stirred up that element in the community which is linked by old memories and associations with the border days, when the people of this country were divided on the issues of the civil war. Old men with excited faces and eyes flashing with anger appeared at police headquarters and around the jail early this morning and demanded to know where Jesse James was and by what authority he was held. The voices of these men trembled with excitement as they talked about the case.

"At the court house the police were denounced for arresting James. Many of the people employed there made light of the police claim that they had a strong case, and it was evident that Jesse James, guilty or guiltless, had friends there. The arrest was spoken of by some as a very serious mistake, for it would be 'bad for the party.'

JUDGE HENRY CALLS IT AN OUTRAGE

Judge Henry was very indignant at the manner in which Jesse James had been arrested. He said to a reporter for The Star this morning:

"The manner in which this boy was kidnapped by the police was a damnable outrage. You must bear in mind that young Jesse James is not like other boys. He occupies a peculiar position in this community. His father was a bandit and was killed for a reward. Young Jesse has grown up here, watched by everybody. Many watched over him with solicitude for his welfare, advising him, guiding his footsteps in the right, anxious for him to get along and be a good, clean man.

"Many others watched him askance to see how soon he would show a tendency to follow in his father's footsteps. Many wished him ill. I have watched this boy closely. I know that no boy in the county has led a cleaner life. He has worked and slaved and saved, and alone and unaided has paid for the home in which he, his mother and sister live. It was his wages that clothed his sister and paid for her music lessons. No one ever saw this boy in a saloon. Who ever saw him out late at night? "Who ever heard of him being in a brawl or scandal? Here he has grown up with us, with his father's past to live down, and I say he has shown himself a well balanced, worthy boy.

"To brand that boy as a train robber, if he were innocent, would be a crime that would merit hanging. So I say that the police should have waited till they were sure he was guilty, and then they should have gone in open daylight and sworn out a warrant and arrested him, and placed him in jail so that his mother and sister could see him. Instead of that they kidnap him and hide him away. That is evidence to me that they do not know he is guilty. They kidnap him to put the thumb-screws upon him in secret and try and extort something from him. That is unlawful and unfair."

"Chief Hayes said this afternoon that Jesse James was not even locked up last night. He was kept in a well furnished room, and was allowed to telephone to his mother and to his friends.

The chief said he had talked very little to him about the case during the night.

HAD A RIGHT TO KILL THE OFFICERS

Finis C. Farr, lawyer for Jesse James, said: 'The grand jury has been in session for weeks. If the police have evidence against the boy why didn't they have him indicted. Jesse knew they were shadowing him. He had no intention of running away. He was tending his cigar stand in the courthouse when he was kidnapped. Why did the police spirit him away unless it was to bulldoze and browbeat him into saying something that would hurt him? That is the Pinkerton way of doing things: It was the Pinkertons who threw the bomb into the house of this boy's grandmother and blew her arm off and killed her baby. The Pinkertons hate the whole James family. But I'll tell you they can't kidnap people in this community with impunity, no matter whether they are train robbers or not. Jesse had a right to kill those officers who took him without a warrant and he ought to have done it."

R. L. YEAGER AS HIS LAWYER

R. L. Yeager, a lawyer and president of the school board, went to see Chief Hayes this morning and demanded that Jesse James be released within an hour. Mr. Yeager said:

"I have been employee to defend Jesse James, who was kidnapped by the police unlawfully. He must be released or properly apprehended and held.

"Ex-Governor T. T. Crittenden said: 'The arrest of Jesse James is a greater crime than train robbery. If I were governor I would have the men who arrested him indicted.'

The Star said of my arrest upon this day:

JESSE James's good record

Jesse James' friends—and the young man has many, some of them among the responsible citizens of the town—are loth to believe the suspicions gathering about him. He has always been known as a steady, industrious and home-loving youth, fond of his mother, and willing to be guided by her wishes. To his mother any suggestion that Jesse has been guilty of wrong will come as a heavy blow. The same may be said of his grandmother, the aged Mrs. Samuels, who lives near Kearney. Mrs. Samuels lives in talking and thinking of her boy Jesse, and Jesse, jr., she idolizes, but, although her son was a bandit, she would not have Jesse, jr., go the same way. Jessie never has looked upon his father as the criminal that the world pictures him, yet the fact that there is a stain upon his father's name has always served as a governor in his actions. His employers liked him and always spoke in the highest terms of his steadiness and unremitting application to duty. They say, too, that during the several years he was stock taker in the cured meat department he never was caught in a mistake. His salary was not large, but it sufficed for the modest needs of the family of three, and by careful economy permitted the saving of the money that paid for the home at 3402 Tracy Avenue."

Later on in the day I was admitted to bond in the sum of $2,500, furnished by E. F. Swinney, cashier of the First National Bank, and Finis C. Farr.

CHAPTER XI. THE TRIAL FOR TRAIN ROBBERY

My trial on a charge of being the leader of the band which held up the train at Leeds began in the criminal court of Jackson County, Mo., February 23, 1899. Of the five cases against men under arrest and indictment for this robbery, my case was selected for trial first, although I was many years younger than any of the others and had a reputation in the community that was spoken of by all the newspapers as good. The prosecution claimed that my case was selected for trial first because I was the planner of the robbery and the leader of the band. I believe that my case was selected for trial first because there was no case against any of the other men who were indicted for this robbery except W. W. Lowe, who confessed this robbery. My theory of the conspiracy to convict me is that Lowe actually was in this robbery, that his wife, who was anxious to get rid of him, informed the detectives, and he was at once arrested and very damaging evidence accumulated against him by the detectives. I believe that every pressure that the ingenuity of the detectives could devise was brought to bear on him to make him confess who his accomplices were, but he steadfastly refused to confess, owing to some sense of honor that he might have had or because he was afraid that his accomplices might kill him if he did confess. The detectives then, either by inference or by direct statements made to him, gave him to understand that they believed I was in the robbery. Lowe saw by their statements that the detectives were anxious to fasten the crime on me. Lowe then intimated that I was in the robbery, and at once the detectives promised him immunity if he would confess, and not only that, but Del Harbaugh, the Missouri Pacific detective, promised that his case would be dismissed and he given a good position on the Missouri Pacific railroad if he would tell all. Lowe then confessed, not all at once, but piecemeal, that I was with him in the robbery. Of course he had to give the names of others who were in the robbery too, and he selected the names of men known to be acquainted with me. They were Andy Ryan, Charles Polk and Caleb Stone. Andy Ryan I had known almost from my infancy, owing to the fact that he lived in Kansas City and was a member in good standing of the city fire department, and as his brother. Bill Ryan, had been an acquaintance of my father, I came naturally to know Andy Ryan, and I never knew wrong of him. Andy Ryan was by no means an associate of mine; I simply had a passing acquaintance with him. Polk I knew very well. He worked at Armor's packing house when I worked there. I had a little acquaintance with Caleb Stone, an old man of seventy years. The detectives knew that I knew all of these men, and in casting about in their minds for men to associate with me in Lowe's false confession of the train robbery, they probably selected these men almost at haphazard, simply because they knew that I knew them. Certain it is that not a scrap of evidence was ever produced to show that Ryan, Polk or Stone had the slightest connection with the Leeds robbery, and they were discharged from custody as soon as I was acquitted.

My theory as to why the detectives sought to convict me of the robbery, takes in several causes and motives on their part. There had been a number of train robberies recently in Jackson County. The detectives were unable to capture the robbers. The railroad companies who employed these detectives, were naturally dissatisfied with their failure to do so. This incensed the detectives. When Harbaugh was brought into the case a man came who was wholly unscrupulous. He was found not to fail. He would catch someone. Harbaugh knew that if he could convict Jesse James for the robbery, after the failure of all the detectives who had gone before him and failed to convict anyone, it would win him a great reputation. This is why he sought, by a conspiracy, to convict me.

The detectives even claimed that a man named Jennings, who was in jail at Springfield, was really Bill Ryan, and that Bill Ryan was in the robbery at Leeds. The detectives knew this to be absolutely false. Jennings is not Bill Ryan.

The reader who will take the trouble to follow the trial as I will outline it here, will see how this theory of mine is borne out by the facts as they developed, and at the end of the trial, which resulted in my acquittal, the reader will see the cases against all of the other men dismissed, and even Lowe was allowed to walk, a free man, out of the court room.

As bearing out my theory of the conspiracy to convict me, I quote as follows from the Kansas City Star of October 12, 1898:

"Lowe was kept locked up. He was continually harassed by detectives, who plied him with questions. Lowe is a Free Mason, and so is Harbaugh, the detective. Harbaugh promised Lowe that if he would confess he would guarantee that he would be given the lowest penalty; his child would be put in the Free Masons home and cared for while he was in the penitentiary, and when his term was up he would be given a permanent job on the railroad, Lowe has a brother who is an engineer on the Missouri Pacific railroad and the detectives sent for him and had him urge Lowe to make a confession. Then Lowe confessed that Jesse James was in the robbery."

The twelve jurors who heard my trial and returned a verdict of acquittal, were King R. Powell, William Ewing, Albert L. Miller, Eugene McEntee, John J. Durrett, William S. Rodgers, Leonard Veugelen, Samuel E. Spence, Joseph M. McConnell, William E. Mullens, J. E. Broughal and Harry G. Clark.

Of these jurors the Star of February 22, 1899, said:

"The jurors are regarded as excellent men, who will do their duty as their consciences see if."

The Journal of the same date said; "Neither side has been able to find a blemish upon the name and character of any of the jurymen."

The Kansas City World of February 23 said:

"Both sides consider the jury an exceptionally fine one. Every man on it resides in Kansas City and is apparently a man of more than ordinary intelligence.'

'While the jurors were being selected in the court room, it developed that detectives had questioned them and attempted to influence them against me.

My lawyers were Frank P. Walsh, Finis C. Farr, R. L. Yeager, president of the Kansas City school board, and Milton J. Oldham. The magnificent management of my case is due to the skill, ability and legal learning of these four splendid men.

The county prosecutor who represented the state at the trial was James A. Reed, and he was assisted by Frank G. Johnson.

Of the interest which my trial excited, the Kansas City Star said during its progress:

"In all the history of criminal courts in this country there has probably never been a trial in which there was so much strained attention by the spectators in the court room to every word and to everything done, as there is in the trial of Jesse James for train robbery, now on in the criminal court here. There have been many trials in which the public took a deep interest. In this same court room a woman was tried for her life not long ago; it was a most interesting trial and the court room overflowed day after day. There have been other remarkable trials. But in all these other trials the court room filled with a hodge-podge audience of all sorts of persons, who seemed to have come from mere curiosity and you've ready to laugh at the most trivial thing.

"But in this trial of Jesse James every one of the hundreds in the court room seems to have a personal interest in it. They watch things so closely. The feelings of suspense that seem to fill the very air of the crowded room, the looks of deep and attentive concern on every face, are quite wonderful to see. There is no levity, no laughter, and there are no interruptions.

"This deep interest is probably because of the fact that the young man on trial is the son of Jesse James, the old rough riding bandit who kept the newspapers of the country well filled with news of his doings hereabouts for a good many years, and it is a thing quite remarkable that this young man, if he is guilty, should have taken up the desperate calling of his father. It is equally remarkable, if this son of a bandit is innocent, and the victim of a gigantic conspiracy on the part of the authorities either to hang him or send him to the penitentiary.

"The jurors seem to be more deeply interested in the trial than jurors usually are in cases they are trying. They do not miss a word or an act of the proceedings. They are thought by court house officials to be jurymen of average intelligence and probable integrity. There are four old men on the jury with gray hair and beards. None of the other eight men appear to be more than forty nor less than twenty-five years old.

"If Jesse James is innocent, he is the victim of one of the most gigantic conspiracies ever concocted to convict a man."

The proceedings on the first day of the trial were reported as follows in the Kansas City Star. I prefer to use the newspaper accounts of the trial because I cannot then be accused of making misrepresentations:

William W. Lowe the principal witness against Jesse James in his trial on the charge of robbing a Missouri Pacific train near Leeds on the night of September 23 last, was on the witness stand in the criminal court all yesterday afternoon and a part of this forenoon. Lowe told how he had known Jack Kennedy and Andy Ryan for many years when Lowe lived in Independence, and they lived near there. He told about meeting Kennedy here in Kansas City last winter, and said he was an alibi witness for Kennedy in Krueger's court, and that Jesse James was a witness there for Kennedy, too; that Lowe and Jesse met there for the first time, became acquainted and kept up this acquaintance, which led up to the train robbery.

Lowe told every detail of the robbery with great minuteness, giving little incidents, such as whom they met, what routes they traveled, what conversations were held, and every little thing that was done. They planned first to rob the train in the early part of September, lie said, but Jesse postponed it because his uncle was in town then. They planned it next for September 21, but it rained hard that day and it was postponed again.

Lowe said that while planning the robbery he was at the home of Jesse James several times, and the night of the robbery the party started from near there. He described the interior of the James home and drew with a pencil before the jury what purported to be a plan of the interior of the place. He said there were in the robbery himself, Jesse James, Andy Ryan, a man who was called Evans, who was a stranger to him, whom he had never seen before or since, and two other men, one an old man, who were introduced to him by Jesse ; they were called Charlie and Harry.

The police claim that the man Evans was Bill Ryan, in jail at Springfield for the Macomb robbery, and that the men called Charlie and Harry were old Caleb Stone and Charles Polk, both under indictment now. But Lowe would not identify Caleb Stone yesterday in the court room. That was a dramatic incident of the trial. It was during the cross-examination of Lowe by Mr. Walsh, lawyer for Jesse James. Caleb Stone sat at the end of the lawyer's table, right behind Jesse James, and facing Lowe and the jury.

"Whom do you say were in this robbery with you besides Jesse James, Ryan and Evans?" asked Walsh.

"Two men called Charlie and the 'Old man.'"

"Describe them."

"Charlie was about my size."

"What sort of a looking man was the "Old man"?

"He was an oldish man."

"Would you know him if you saw him again?"

"I don't know."

Mr. Walsh turned to where Caleb Stone sat and said:

"Stand up, Mr. Stone."

Caleb Stone stood up and looked sharply at Lowe. He is an old man, small in size, bent and slightly stoop shouldered, with gray mustache and chin whiskers, and rather plainly dressed.

"Is that the man?" asked Walsh.

Lowe merely glanced at Stone, and said:

"I wouldn't identify him."

"Do you think it's he?"

"I wouldn't say."

"Does it look like the man?"

"I can't say; I don't know."

"You saw the 'old man' plainly the night of the robbery, did you not?"

"I saw him there."

"Did he have a mask on?"

"No."

"And you don*t know whether this is the man or not?"

"No."

"Why did you go into a robbery with three men you did not know, and had never seen before?"

"Jesse told me they were all right, and Jack Kennedy told me I could bank on anything Jesse said, because he was all right."

Another interesting point in the trial late last evening was when Mr. Walsh asked Lowe why he confessed to the police.

"I refused for fourteen days to tell a thing. They tried to get me to tell, but I wouldn't. I waited for these men who were in the robbery with me to help me out, and I waited fourteen days in jail and they never did a thing for me. I made up my mind that they had 'ditched me,' and I was up against it anyway, and I just told the whole business from start to finish."

A surprising development was when Lowe denied last evening that he had ever made a written confession or statement, or had ever signed his name to one.

Mr. Walsh had a copy of The Star of last October, with Lowe's confession in full printed on the first page. Mr. Walsh questioned him about it, and questioned him again closely this morning. Mr. Walsh read the printed confession. It tallied in every particular with the story told yesterday and today by Lowe on the witness stand. Lowe said when asked about it:

"I never did write down a word about the robbery; I never dictated a statement to a stenographer or to anyone else, and I never signed my name to any statement or confession."

Lowe stuck to it in spite of all questioning, that he never made a written confession or statement.

"I told the police and detectives the whole truth," he declared, "and if they wrote it down that's their business."

"Did they write it down in your presence?"

"No, sir."

The cross-examination of Lowe by Frank P. "Walsh, attorney for Jesse James, gave an idea of what the plan of the defense would be in regard to his testimony. Mr. Walsh questioned Lowe for two hours last evening, and resumed the cross-examination when court opened this morning. It was a very skillful arrangement of questions. The impression sought to be conveyed by these questions was that Lowe was really in the robbery; that after he was arrested the railroad and express companies' detectives and the police tried to get him to confess; that Lowe would not tell anything about it; that they used every inducement they could to get him to confess, promising him immunity and part of the reward, and convincing him that they had him "dead to rights," and threatening to convict him sure unless he confessed; that the detectives kept asking him if he knew Jesse James and Jack Kennedy, and gave him to understand if he would implicate Jesse James in it he would be given immunity; that then Lowe did make an alleged confession, protecting the men who were really in the robbery, and telling that Jesse James, Ryan, Polk and Stone were in it.

"When did you first see any of these detectives?" asked Mr. Walsh.

"One came to my house and represented that he was working for the claim department of the street railway, and that I was witness to an accident on the Twelfth street incline, and that he wanted to talk with me about it. I know right away that he was a detective."

"When did you see him next?"

"When they came to arrest me, some time after that."

"Where did they take you?"

"To the Savoy hotel."

Lowe told this story this morning in answer to questions of how he came to confess to the police:

"They took me from the Savoy to No. 3 police station and locked me up. I was there several days and then they took me to the Westport station. For fourteen days they kept after me, telling me each visit they made the evidence they had against me, and it was good, straight evidence, too. They kept getting after me stronger and stronger all the time. They brought my wife down to see me, and she told me she had told the police all she knew. They "wouldn't let me see an attorney, nor no one else, and they kept telling me what they had again me. Finally I asked to see my brother, and he came and advised me to tell all, and I did so."

"Didn't they promise you immunity?"

"No, sir."

"Didn't they promise you a reward?"

"No, sir."

"Weren't you indicted for this train robbery jointly with Jesse James?"

"I don't know."

"Do you mean to say you don't know?"

"No, I don't know."

"Wasn't a copy of the indictment served on you?"

"It might have been. I don't remember."

"Didn't you know that under that first joint indictment, the state would have to discharge you before you could go on the stand and testify?"

"No I didn't know."

"You know that they had you and Jesse and the others indicted separately afterward, and that now they can use you as a witness without first discharging you?"

"I don't know."

The theory of the defense on this point is that Lowe and Jesse James were indicted separately so that the state could use the indictment as a club over Lowe's head to force him to testify.

"Where have you boarded in Westport since your arrest?" asked Walsh.

"I've taken my meals at the Harris house."

"Haven't you gone out bird hunting since your arrest?"

"I went down the railroad track with an officer. I had a little cartridge gun and was shooting grasshoppers."

"Did Detective Harbaugh tell you that a reward was offered for the conviction of the robbers or one of them, and that he would divide it with you?"

"No, sir."

"Didn't they promise you immunity?"

"No, sir."

"Didn't Chief Hayes advise you to confess?"

"Yes."

"Did he make any promises?"

"He said if I would confess it would go light with me. He said he would make no promises except that he would use his influence. My brother came and advised me to tell it all, too."

"Didn't the officers keep asking you before you confessed, if you knew Jesse James?"

"Yes; they asked me once and I told them I knew him."

"Didn't they tell you they had evidence against Jesse James and Jack Kennedy?"

"No: I think not."

"When you first told about this robbery, did you tell the names of all who were in it?"

"Yes."

Mr. Walsh here began a new series of questions on a point which the defense thinks is a strong one in its favor.

"Who was it took the stuff out of the safe that night after you had set off the dynamite?" '

"The man they called Evans."

"Evans is the alias of the man supposed to be Bill Ryan.

"Did he get any money out of the car?"

"I saw him get packages out."

"How big packages?"

Lowe pointed to two law books on a table and said "As big as the two of them together."

"You say that several times before this robbery you stood at the Union depot and saw them transferring money packages from an Omaha express car to this one you robbed?"

"I said I saw them transfer packages I thought was money."

"Was the package Evans took out' the same shape and size?"

"Yes; it looked just like it."

"What did Evans do with the package he took from the safe?"

"Put it in a sack."

"How big a sack?"

"About a two bushel sack."

"What did he do then?"

"He swung the sack over his shoulder and left."

"Did he go with you?"

"No."

"Do you suppose it was money he got in that package?"

"Yes."

"And you had never seen this man Evans before in your life?"

"No."

"And never since?"

"No."

"And you didn't know who he was?"

"No."

"You let a stranger walk away with what you thought was the money after you had risked so much to rob the train?"

"I supposed he was all right."

Mr. Walsh questioned Lowe further about what occurred at and near the home of Jesse James when Lowe went there the night of the robbery. Lowe said he went to the house and inquired of Jesse's sister for Jesse. She told Lowe he had gone to put his aunt, Mrs. Palmer, on a street car to go to the Union depot. Lowe sat down on the porch and in a little while Jesse came in the back door and called him out to the back and pointed to a clump of trees and said the horse was tied there and for him to go over. Lowe went and found the horse, which was restless. Lowe unhitched the horse and drove it around the block. Jesse came and said he had been to a drug store to show himself, so as to fix an alibi. Jesse and Lowe started in the buggy and picked up Andy Ryan at Thirty-fifth street. They drove out a ways and caught up to the other two men in a buggy. One of these said everything was all right, the big man meaning Evans, would be out at the scene of the robbery.

That ended the cross-examination by Mr. Walsh. Prosecutor Reed asked Lowe if he and Jesse and Ryan talked on the drive back to town about the money got in the robbery.

"Yes," said Lowe; "Ryan told me they didn't get anything. He said too much dynamite was used and it blew everything to the devil. I told him I didn't believe Evans got nothing. I believed he got something."

Lowe said that he went to the jail last August, when this robbery was planned, in response to a letter from Kennedy.

"Is this the letter?" asked Mr. Reed, handing him an envelope and letter.

"Yes, sir; that's it."

The letter was shown to the jury. The envelope was addressed in ink: "Mr. Bill Lowe, 1001 West Sixteenth street, Kansas City, Mo." It was stamped and had passed through the mail and had been delivered to Lowe: It bore the postmark: "Kansas City, Mo., August 15, 10 P. M., '98. The letter was written with a lead pencil on a sheet of note paper and was as follows: 8:15, '98. K. C, Mo.

Mr. Wilum Lowe

Dear friend I thought at i wuld write you a few lines unce for the first time say bil when you get this please cum down if you can.

yours as ever

J. F. Kennedy

This is important evidence for the state if it is actually proved to be Kennedy's writing. The lawyers for the defense realized this and examined the letter closely. Mr. Farr showed it to Major Blake L. Woodson, who had once defended Kennedy on a charge of train robbery and was in the court room. Woodson said he thought it was not Kennedy's writing.

Prosecutor Reed showed Lowe a card on the back of which this was written:

"We the masked knights of the road robbed the Missouri Pacific at the Belt Line junction tonight. The supply of quails was good. With much love, we remain, John Kennedy, Bill Ryan, Bill Anderson, Sam Brown, Jim Redmond. We are ex com spect to."

This card was handed to the express messenger by one of the robbers the night of the robbery. Prosecutor Reed asked Lowe:

"Did you ever see that card before?"

"Yes."

"Where?"

"The Sunday night before the robbery we were at Andy Ryan's house and Jesse showed me that very card."

Edwin E. Hills, the express messenger who was held up, was the next witness, and part of his testimony was quite dramatic. He told what has never been made public before—exactly how much money was on the express car and how much the robbers got. It has always been a matter of speculation with the public as to how much was stolen that night. Hills, the messenger says they got only $30. Hills is a man of about thirty, with a sandy mustache. He talked in a very loud tone, giving straight, direct answers to questions. He said he was in charge of the express car the night of the robbery. Then he went on:

"As we stopped at the Belt Line crossing the night of the robbery I heard some talk outside and a flag signal of five blasts. I heard the word 'injector' spoken outside the car. In a minute or two the car started again and I noticed it was not the usual motion of the train. I looked out and saw the balance of the train behind us and just the express car attached to the engine. I made up my mind we were being held up. I got my shot gun and laid it on my box and hid my personal valuables. The car stopped and some one knocked on the door and with an oath, said:

"Open the door or we'll blow your car to hell.'

"I parleyed with them and looked out. I saw the forms of several men. I heard some one say: 'We'll get the dynamite and blow him up.' I told them never mind, boys, I'll open up. They ordered me to put up my hands. I put them up. One climbed up and ordered me back in the end of the car. Another got in."

Hills told about how they placed the little safe on top of the dynamite on the big safe and blew it up, and tried to make him stay in the car when the explosion occurred. He described the explosion, which knocked him flat where he stood by the engine. He said as the robbers left one of them handed him a card.

Prosecutor Reed showed him the card introduced in evidence a short time before, and identified by Lowe. Hills said:

"The leader handed me that card and told me to show it to the newspapers in the morning."

"Describe the leader, the one who got in the car and did so much talking," said Prosecutor Reed.

"He had on a black mask, dark coat like a mackintosh, that came almost to his heels and he carried a double barreled shot gun when he first got in the car."

"What money did you have in the car that night?"

"One sack of silver with $1,000 in it, a package of $590 in currency, two C. 0. D. packages containing $18 and two packages of government war bonds, amounting to $560."

"How much of this was recovered?"

"All but thirty dollars of the silver dollars, which were lost. The other packages were recovered intact.

"Did you get a good chance to observe the leader who was in the car with you?"

"The best chance I had was while he was in the rear of the car, where the light was quite dim. He wore a black mask of glazed oilcloth."

Prosecutor Reed showed the glazed mask found in the weeds near the scene of the robbery and identified by Lowe yesterday as very much like the one worn by Jesse James. Hills said it was like the one worn by the leader.

"Describe the leader's appearance."

"He was a small man, five feet six or seven inches tall, weighing one hundred and thirty to one hundred and forty-five or one hundred and fifty pounds. He had very sharp, piercing eyes, and a nose rather prominent."

At the request of Prosecutor Reed, Jesse James stood up and looked, without a trace of nervousness, straight at the witness.

"How did the leader's height compare with the height of the defendant?" asked Prosecutor Reed.

"'I should say he was about the same height."

"How does he compare as to breadth of shoulders?"

"About the same. He bore a general resemblance to the man who just stood up."

"You say you noticed the leader's. How does the defendant's eyes compare with them?"

"The robber's eyes were large and piercing eyes, as this man has."

"Is the defendant the man that was there that night and wore the coat and mask?"

"I am unable to state."

Hills then told the following story, giving it with good dramatic gestures, imitations and general effect:

"The next afternoon after the robbery I went to the court house to get a good look at Jesse James and see if he was the man who held me up."

"Who told you to go?"

"Superintendent Moore of the Pacific Express."

"Tell what occurred."

"I went in the court house and Jesse was not there. I strolled around and soon he came in and went behind his cigar stand. I walked up and looked him square in the eye and said:

"I want a cigar."

"I looked square into his eyes and he dropped his eyes and raised them and dropped them again. I found fault with the cigar he handed me and said:

"Young man, I was out late last night and I'm a little nervous. I want a nice, mild cigar to settle my nerves.

"He reached in and got one and I paid him. As he handed me the change he said in a deep tone of voice:

"Thank you, sir.' "

"Did his voice resemble any you had ever heard before?"

"No; it was not his natural voice even."

Court adjourned for noon at this point.

After the court adjournment at noon Frank P. Walsh, attorney for Jesse James, was asked what he thought of the testimony of W. W. Lowe. He said:

"The most important thing for the defense is that Lowe now denies positively that he ever made a written confession; that he ever dictated a confession, or that he ever signed his name to any statement whatever. When we showed him his confession published in the Star, October 13, he said it was not his, that he never made it, but we will prove that Lowe did make the confession printed in the Star of that date.

"The reason Lowe denies that confession now is because there are discrepancies between his confession and his testimony now. For instance, there is a discrepancy in the time he says he left the point near the James home to go to the robbery, and there is a discrepancy between his statements with regard to where he met Evans.

"In his printed confession he says he met the big man Evans near the James home. He says he, Jesse and Andy Ryan got in one buggy and Charlie, the 'old man' and Evans got in another buggy, and all drove out together. Now he swears that he and Jesse got in the buggy and drove out and overtook Andy and they drove on and overtook Charlie and the 'old man' in another buggy, and that the first time he saw Evans was after he got to the scene of the robbery.

"Another thing, Lowe denied positively yesterday afternoon that he had been promised anything to confess. I asked him positively yesterday if the police promised to be light on him if he confessed. He said, "No." This morning he admits that this promise was made to him."

Prosecutor Reed was asked today why Lowe denied his confession.

"Why," said Mr. Reed, **he never did make a written confession, and never did sign one. He told the officers, I suppose, the whole truth, and they wrote it down in a condensed form, and that is what The Star printed."

When court met after the noon recess today, Hills, the messenger, was put on the witness stand again and was asked by Prosecutor Reed:

"Did you ever hear the voice of Jesse James at any other time than when you were at his cigar stand?"

"Yes, sir."

"Where?"

"At the Westport police station."

"Where did you ever hear that voice before?"

"The night of the robbery."

"Whose voice was it?"

"The voice of the leader of the gang."

Charles A. Slocum, engineer of the train that was held up, was called next. He said they got to Belt Line crossing about 9:59 or 10 o'clock. The train stopped at the crossing. A man stepped up to the engine cab with a gun. He told them to get down and they did so and held up their hands. The man who ordered them down had an Irish brogue. One of the men on the ground said to another:

"All right. Bill, get up in the engine."

"The man called Bill got up in the cab and blew five blasts on the engine whistle as a signal for the brakeman to go out behind with a flag."

"Had William W. Lowe ever worked with you before, Mr. Slocum?" asked Prosecutor Reed.

"Yes, sir."

"Did you get a good look at the robber who climbed up in your cab?"

"Yes, sir."

"Was he William W. Lowe?'"

"Yes, sir; it was William W. Lowe."

Slocum told the story of how the baggage car was uncoupled, and all that was done, his story agreeing in every particular with the testimony of W. W. Lowe and Hills, the express messenger.

"Did you get a good look at the man who marched the express messenger out at the point of a gun?"

"No; I didn't see him closely."

"Describe him as near as you can."

"He weighed about one hundred and thirty five or one hundred and forty pounds and slim built, and wore a long coat nearly down to his heels."

Jesse James stood up at the request of the prosecutor, but Mr. Walsh objected to Slocum giving his opinion, because Slocum had said all he knew was that it was a slim man. The court sustained this objection.

"What sort of a looking man was the one who guarded you at the engine?"

"He talked with an Irish brogue and had a peculiar way of throwing his head forward, and he talked in a nice, easy tone."

"Have you seen that man since?"

"I couldn't say positively."

Slocum had been taken to Mansfield to see Bill Ryan, under arrest there for robbing a Memphis train. The theory of the state is that Bill Ryan was the Evans of the Leeds hold-up, but Slocum would not say that the Evans of the Leeds hold-up was the man under arrest at Mansfield.

"What is your best judgment about it?"

"I do not know positively."

Prosecutor Reed pressed the question and Walsh objected. The judge finally interfered and asked Slocum:

"Now, sir, if you saw that man again would you recognize him?"

"If I saw him act and heard his voice I could probably say."

"Have you seen the man since?"

"I have seen a man who answers very well the description of that man."

"Did you recognize him as the same man?"

"I wouldn't say positively."

Prosecutor Reed asked: "Where did you see that man?"

"At Mansfield, but I would not swear positively it was the same, but he tallies well with the same man."

Mr. Walsh, in cross examining Slocum, asked: "Did you know positively that it was W. W. Lowe when he got in the engine that night?"

"I thought it was him."

"Did he call you by name, or you call him?"

"No."

"How long had Lowe worked for you before that."

"He had fired for me at different times."

"Will you swear positively that it was William W. Lowe who held you up that night?"

Mr. Slocum hit the arm of the witness chair very vigorously with his clinched fist as he answered:

"I made up my mind right then that it was Lowe, and I haven't changed it since."

"When did you first tell that it was Lowe?"

"About two days after the robbery I told it to Del Harbaugh, the detective. I think I told my fireman, too."

"Were you trying to conceal that you recognized Lowe?"

"I didn't want to say anything to hurt him. I didn't want to cause him trouble."

E. L. Weston, fireman of the train, testified next and his story of the details of how the train was held up agree with the stories told by Lowe, Hills and Slocum. Mr. Walsh asked him on cross examination:

"Do you know W. W. Lowe?"

"Yes; I've known him for ten years."

"Was Lowe the man who got into the cab?"

"I don't know."

"Did you see Lowe there that night?"

"I don't know."

Weston testified that he had been to Mansfield and saw the man under arrest there and thought it was one of the men who was at the engine the night of the robbery, but would not say it was the same.

Line junction, who was captured by the robbers, was the next witness. He said he was leaning back in his chair in the telegraph shanty and a man came in and with an oath ordered him to throw up his hands. Another man came in and smashed the telegraph instruments with a pair of pliers.

Prosecutor Reed showed him the pliers which were found the next morning on the ground, and Hisey said they were the same. Hisey said the man who held him up had a shot gun and shoved it in his face and cursed and was very fierce, threatening to kill him. There was a man in the office waiting to get a ride on a freight train, and the robbers held him up, too, and marched both of them down to where the rest of the gang had held up the train. One of the two robbers who took him from the shanty called the other Bill.

"The man who held me up had a light hat on, a black mask with the eyes showing and a long rubber coat nearly to his heels. I heard it rattle. I saw his chin. He was a small man, who would weigh one hundred and forty or one hundred and forty-five pounds, a young fellow. He swore nearly every word he said.

"Have you seen the man since who held you up that night?" asked Prosecutor Reed.

"I have seen a man I think is him."

"Who is he?"

Hisey pointed straight at Jesse James and said positively:

"That fellow sitting right there."

"Who, Jesse James?"

"Yes; Jesse James. I think he is undoubtedly the fellow; there is no mistake about it."

This was by all odds the strongest evidence against Jesse James produced at the trial so far. It amounts almost to a positive identification. Jesse James did not flinch under it or show signs of nervousness.

Hisey testified further that he saw Jesse James in the Westport jail after the robbery and he noticed the moment he went in that Jesse watched him. He saw Jesse at the court house and said to him there:

"I have been mistaken about the color of your eyes. It looked to me as if you had dark eyes, but I see now that they are light. It seemed that they were dark when you had that mask on."

Mr. Walsh, in cross-examining Hisey, asked this question:

"Didn't you say in Witte's saloon, in Leeds, a month after this robbery, that it was not Jesse James who held you up?"

"No, sir."

"Didn't you say, in the presence of Murphy, Mason, Miller, Noland and others, in that saloon, that you had seen Jesse James since the robbery and it was not Jesse who held you up?"

"No, sir; I did not."

The Star of February 25 printed the following:

"The most positive identification of Jesse James as one of the Leeds train robbers was made in the court room this afternoon by William J. Smith of Stotesbury, Missouri, who was a passenger on the Missouri Pacific train the night it was held up. Smith testified that he was riding in the smoking car and got out when the train was held up and walked up among the robbers. One of the robbers put a gun against his breast and ordered him back into the car.

"Did that man have anything over his face?" asked Prosecutor Reed.

"He had nothing over his face. He had something black around his neck, as if it were a mask, slipped down."

"How light was it?"

"It was very light. The light streamed out the mail car door."

"Did you get a good look at that man!"

"Yes, sir; I got a good look at him."

"Do you see that man in the court room?"

Mr. Smith pointed to Jesse James, sitting facing him and said:

"Yes, sir; there he sits right over there,"

"You mean the defendant, Jesse James?"

"Yes, sir; it was Jesse James."

Frank P. Walsh began the cross-examination of Smith.

"Where were you born?"

"In Kentucky."

"How long have you lived in Stotesbury?"

"Two years."

"Where did you live before that?"

"On a farm in Cass county."

"How long did you farm there?"

"Eleven years."

Mr. Walsh volleys him with questions about Detective Harbaugh and other detectives. He asked if Harbaugh had been with you a good deal lately. Smith said that he first saw Harbaugh a month ago when Harbaugh went to his home in Stotesbury with Detective Bryant to see what he knew. Smith said he was staying here with his brother-in-law, E. T. Bergen, who drives a hack for the Depot Carriage company. He said that detectives were not paying his way here, but he expected his expenses to be paid for coming here to testify. He said Harbaugh was not paying him. Smith said he was working for the Pittsburg & Gulf railroad.

The next day of the trial this fellow Smith was put on the stand and had to admit that he had been in jail for burglary and that for the sake of his family his friends bailed him out. Scarcely anyone in the court room believed any part of the testimony of Smith.

The Star's account of the rest of the testimony this day was as follows:

"S. M. Downer, a freight conductor on the Missouri Pacific, testified that Sunday, August 28, while his train was coming to Kansas City two men boarded it when the train stopped at the Belt Line crossing. They got on midway of the train and climbed on top of a car. Downer sent his rear brakeman up to tell them to get off. The two men walked back over the top of the train to the caboose. The larger one clambered into the caboose and the other stayed outside. The man who went in said:

"Mr. Downer, I'm a railroad man, I'm switching in the Santa Fe yards. I've been out here to a Dutch picnic in Swope park and if I don't get in on your train I 'll be too late for my work."

Downer asked him his name and he said it was Bill Lowe. That started a conversation, because Downer knew Lowe's brother.

"Who was with Lowe?" asked Prosecutor Reed.

"A young man of twenty-three or twenty-four years, smooth faced, weighing from one hundred and thirty-five to one hundred and fifty pounds."

"Do you think you would recognize him if you saw him?"

"I have seen the young man since, but I won't swear to it.'" answered Downer.

Judge Shackleford asked Downer: "Could you be reasonably certain of this young man if you saw him?"

"Yes," answered Downer.

"Now, Mr. Reed, you may ask him who it was," said the judge.

"Who was it?" asked Reed.

"I think it was that young man sitting there," pointing to Jesse James.

"You mean Mr. James?"

"Yes, sir; Mr. James."

Mr. Walsh cross-examined Downer:

"Did you get a good look at the young man who was with Lowe?"

"No; I only glanced at him as he was crossing the car next to the caboose."

"On such a slight glance are you willing to swear that Jesse James was the man?"

"I haven't done so."

"You don't want to swear this young man is the one?"

If I answer in this way, to my best judgment. I say he is the one, but I will not swear positively to if.

The next three witnesses were T. H. Hutchison, a grocer and a school director of Leeds, who swore that Sunday, August 28, W. W. Lowe and Jesse James called at his store; Walter Hutchinson, his son, who saw Jesse and Lowe there, and Burt Meyers, a young man who saw them, too.

T. H. Hutchison said he became acquainted with Jesse James last July, when Jesse went to him to try and get a place for his listen to teach school.

"I was in my store August 28 when Jesse and another man came in. a little after one o'clock and asked for a drink. I drew a fresh bucket of water. They talked awhile. The big man pointed to a shot gun on the wall and said it was like one his father used to own. When they were leaving Jesse asked me who got the school. I told him and he said it was just as he had expected. They went south in the direction of Belt Line junction."

W. Lowe was brought into the court room and Mr. Hutchison pointed to him and said: "That is the man who was with Jesse."

Walter Hutchison and Bert Meyers swore that they were at the store when Jesse and the other man were there, but they could not say that the other man was Lowe.

Francis McGingan, a coal miner, said he went to the scene of the hold-up the next morning and found false whiskers. He was shown those in the court room and identified them.

The next three witnesses were Will Starkey, Ben Shaeffer and A. J. Theakston. They were working for the Missouri Valley Bridge Company Sunday, August 28, finishing a new bridge for the 'Frisco road near Leeds and near where the train was held up. Starkey knew Jesse James, because Starkey boarded with one of the school directors and Jesse had been out there to try to get a place for his sister to teach school. Starkey testified that Sunday afternoon, August 28, he saw Jesse James and another man walking on the Missouri Pacific tracks near where the hold-up was. He pointed out Jesse to the other workmen on the bridge. Shaeffer and Theakston corroborated this and had their time books in court to prove that they did work on that bridge that afternoon.

There was one witness that the state did not call and he was H. P. Vallee, the brakeman of the train upon which Lowe said he and I rode in from Leeds. Soon after my arrest I secured the following affidavit from Vallee:

"H. P. Vallee, of lawful age, being duly sworn, upon his oath says that he is in the employ of the Missouri Pacific railroad as brakeman on a freight train; that he was acting in that capacity on the freight train on that road known as second No. 208 on the 28th day of August, 1898, when W. W. Lowe and another man rode on that train from the Pittsburg and Gulf crossing to Sheffield on that line; that S. M. Downer was the conductor of the train; that I have seen and conversed with Jesse James today and am positive that he was not the man who was on the train with Lowe on that occasion; nor have I ever said or intimated that he was, but "upon the contrary I have at all times since I was first asked to look at James and identify him said that he was not the man. The man who was on the train with Lowe was taller than James and had sandy hair and three or four days growth of sandy beard. I have never seen James on any train at any time."

To show now how the railroad detectives conspired to convict me I wished, of course, to have Vallee as one of my witnesses. He would have been a lost important witness in my behalf. His testimony would have impeached Lowe and proven his story to be false. To prevent my getting him as a witness the railroad company took him away from his job in Missouri and gave him another job as brakeman on their line in Kansas, and told him he would lose his job altogether if he came and testified for me. The law is that a man cannot be compelled to come from one state into another to be a witness in a case. So I was utterly powerless to get Vallee to testify for me. Milton J. Oldham, one of my lawyers, tried to learn from the railroad company the location of Vallee but they refused to tell him.

The day that the state closed its testimony against me the Kansas City Star printed the following:

"The past life and character of Jesse James and his general reputation in this community, where he has lived since he was a child, will be shown by the defense before it closes its side of the case in the trial of Jesse James for train robbery, which defense began in the criminal court this morning. It is likely that this testimony about the good habits of Jesse and his devotion to his widowed mother and his orphaned sister will have as much influence with the jury in reaching a verdict as anything else in the case.

"To look at young Jesse James as he sits day after day in the court room it is hard to believe that he is a train robber or a criminal of any sort. He does not look nor carry himself like the men who rob trains usually do. He is boyish in his looks; he is a boy in his actions. He has nothing of a hardened look on his face. He does not seem to take the trial as a very serious matter. He listens to the important testimony and follows it intently, but in the intervals when questions are asked about things of lesser interest he talks, jokes and laughs with the newspaper reporters and with others and seems to take a boyish interest and delight in any kind of a laughable thing that happens.

"This morning when the trial was in progress and a witness was giving important testimony a young man whom Jesse knew very well entered and sat down close to him. Jesse leaned over and whispered:

"How did the Tigers come out at Lawrence?"

A whispered reply was made and Jesse laughed and asked again:

"Who played guards? Who played in my place?"

Jesse is a member of the Tigers' basket ball team that played the Lawrence team Saturday.

So far, neither the mother, sister nor grandmother—old Mrs. Samuels—of young Jesse James has been in the court room, but they will be there and they will tell what a good boy Jesse has always been. This will be among the most important testimony in behalf of Jesse. It will require strong evidence to convince the average juror that a young man only twenty-two years old, who has been almost the sole support of his mother and his sister since he was eleven years old, who worked through all these boyhood years almost without losing a day, who deprived himself of the things boys love and carried his wages home every payday and gave his earnings to his mother to help pay off the mortgage on the house, and who actually did alone and unaided, pay for this home; it will be hard to make the average juror believe that that boy robbed a train.

When the jurors see the young man's mother on the stand and hear her tell these things; when they hear his sister tell of his love and devotion to her and that it was his wages that kept her at school and gave her a musical education; when the old grandmother tells how kind and devoted this only son of her bandit son has been, it will go a long way with the jury.

And these things are true. Jesse James has been a model son and brother. The people of this community have watched him grow up and until this charge of train robbery was brought against him there was nothing wrong ever heard of him.

I quote the newspaper account again of my defense, as follows:

Cassimer Welsh, a deputy marshal, was sworn and testified.

I and Deputy Marshal Leahy went to the scene of the robbery the night of the robbery and talked to Hills, the express messenger. We asked Hills for a description of the men. He said the man who seemed to be the leader and did all the talking was a big man. We asked him to describe him and just then Sergeant Caskey came in with his uniform on, and Hills pointed to Caskey and said the leader was about the size of him. Hills said the leader was over six feet tall."

"How does Sergeant Caskey compare in size with Jesse James?"

"Caskey is almost twice as large."

"Did Hills at any time describe a man who an answer to a description of Jesse James."

Deputy Welsh answered very positively:

"No, sir; he did not describe anyone who would answer to a description of Jess James."

Charles K. Bowen of the Kansas City View Company, testified that after the arrest of

Jesse James he went with Finis C. Farr, one of Jesse James' lawyers, to the scene of the robbery and talked with Hisey, the telegraph operator who was held up by the robbers.

"I asked Hisey if it was Jesse James who held him up and he told me that it was not Jesse James. He said he had been down to the court house and looked at Jesse, and it was not he who held him up."

Prosecutor Reed, on cross-examination, asked:

"Are you sure Hisey told you it was not Jesse James?"

"I am as positive as that I am sitting here.

Hisey didn't have any reservation. He said he could not tell who it was who held him up and hadn't the least idea who it was."

H. B. Leavins of 3341 Forest avenue, secretary of the Lombard Investment Company, testified that the night of the robbery he saw Jesse James at the south end of the Troost avenue car line at 8:15 o'clock, or very near that time.

Mrs. H. B. Leavins testified that the night of the robbery she and her husband were at the end of the Troost avenue car line and saw Jesse help his mother and another woman and two children on the car.

"What time was that?" she was asked.

"Some time between 8 and 8:30 o'clock, as near as I can tell."

Charles W. Hovey, a deputy county clerk, said that the night of the robbery he saw Jesse James at the drug store at the end of the Troost avenue line at 9 o'clock. He was sure it was 9 o'clock because he heard the curfew whistle blow. Mr. Hovey also testified as follows:

"After Jesse was arrested he came to me and asked me to go over to the city hall with him to see S. M. Downer, conductor of a freight train. I am a notary public and Jesse wanted me to take Downer's affidavit. I took my notarial seal with me. Jesse James asked Downer in my presence and hearing if he had said that he would identify Jesse as the man who rode in with Lowe from Belt Line junction Sunday afternoon, August 28. Downer said he had not said it was Jesse, and he would not say that it was Jesse who was on the train. Jesse asked him to make an affidavit to that effect and Downer said, "No; he had a good job on the Missouri Pacific road and he was not going to lose it by making affidavits."

George TV. Tourtellot, superintendent of the Armor Packing company was the first witness examined after the noon recess and the first witness to the good reputation of Jesse

James.

"How long have you known Jesse James?" was asked him.

"Seven or eight years."

"How long did he work for the Armor Packing company?"

"Six years."

"Are you acquainted with his reputation in this community for honesty, uprightness, truth and veracity?"

"I am."

"What is it?"

"It has been first-class in every respect."

C. E. Jones, a druggist of Thirty-third street and Troost avenue, testified next that Jesse James was in his store the night of the robbery as late as 8:45 o'clock and talked to John Noland, who was playing the slot machine, and that Jesse got some pennies and played the slot machine, too, and was in the store six or eight minutes.

Walter Gaugh, a bookbinder, testified that the night of the robbery he left the junction of Ninth and Main streets at 8:30 o 'clock and went on a cable car to the end of the Troost line and got to the end of the line at 9 o'clock or a little after, and saw Jesse James there.

Charles Howard, of Hill & Howard's drug store at the end of the Troost avenue ear line, testified that Jesse James was in the store at 8:55 o'clock and took a glass of soda water.

"Miss Murray, a stenographer in the New York Life building, was sworn and testified that in November she took the deposition of Hisey, the telegraph operator. She had this deposition with her and said Hisey gave it under oath. The following questions asked Hisey and his answers were read to the jury:

"I will ask you who those two men were that came and held you up, if you know?"

"I was not acquainted with the gentlemen."

"Did you know them at any time?"

"Never met them before to the best of my knowledge."

"Have you ever met them since?"

"I could not say positively that I have, and I could not say positively that I have not. That is a pretty hard question to answer."

This testimony is important as tending to impeach Hisey, who says now that one of the men was Jesse James. When Hisey was on the stand the other day these questions and answers in his deposition were read to him and he denied that he gave the answers.

James S. Rice, a watchman at the end of the Troost line, testified that he saw Jesse James in Hill & Howard's drug store at 9 o'clock. Rice said he came out of the drug store just as the curfew whistle blew, and Jesse James entered the store at the same time.

G. W. Daniels, a Wells-Fargo express messenger, testified next that he saw Jesse James in Hill & Howard's drug store at 9:10 or 9:15 o'clock. Daniels said he was driving north on Troost avenue and was passing J. J. Squires' house, six blocks from the drug store, when the 9 o'clock curfew whistle blew. He drove leisurely to the drug store and saw Jesse in there. Daniels said he told his superintendent about it a few days after the robbery.

Dr. T. J. Beatty testified that he saw Jesse James in the barber shop at Thirty-third street and Troost avenue at seven o 'clock. When the doctor told this Prosecutor Reed asked him with a laugh:

"What time did the curfew whistle blow that night?"

"I don't know."

"You mean to say you didn't hear it."

"I didn't hear it."

"What time did the explosion go off?"

"I don't know."

"Didn't hear that either, hey?"

"No."

Joe Gorsuch, a bill clerk for the Kansas City, Fort Scott & Memphis road, testified that he saw Jesse James at 8:30 o'clock at the end of the Troost avenue line the night of the robbery.

Mrs. Ida Foster lived on the other side of the street from Jesse James and a half block south, at the time of the robbery. She sat at the window till 7:30 o'clock with the trees in plain sight to which W. W. Lowe says the horse used by the robbers was hitched. There was no horse and buggy there up to 7:30 o'clock. She could say nothing about it after that time.

Mrs. O. D. Stanley who lived in the same house with Mrs. Foster, testified that the night of the robbery she sat on her front porch from 7:30 until 9o'clock. The trees to which Lowe says the horse and buggy stood were across the street and in full view and she was sure there was no rig there. On cross examination Mrs. Stanley said her husband came home at 7:30 o'clock that night, and she poured the coffee for him, and she could not remember whether she did or did not stay with him in the house while he ate his supper.

Mrs. J. M. Bunch lives at 3338 Forest avenue, near the James home. The night of the robbery she and her husband were sitting on the steps of their house when Jesse James passed at 9:10 or 9:20 o'clock. They spoke to him and he answered and went on and into his own home. Mrs. Bunch fixed the time because she heard the curfew blow.

J. M. Bunch corroborated this testimony of his wife.

"How did you fix the time that Jesse James went past your house before anyone accused him of anything?" asked Prosecutor Reed.

"Jesse came to see me seven or eight days after the robbery and asked me if I remembered it. He said officers were suspecting him."

At the end of this testimony, which shows that Jesse James was at Thirty-third and Troost as late as 9 o'clock, one of the lawyers of Jesse James whispered to a friend:

"Now you see why W. W. Lowe repudiated his confession printed in The Star. In that confession, it appeared that they started to drive out to rob the train between 8 and 9 o'clock. After Lowe made that confession, the state took all our witnesses before the grand jury and found out that Jesse was at Thirty-third and Troost avenue after 9 o'clock, and so Lowe had to repudiate that first confession and change his testimony to fit with the testimony of ours."

William Cargill, assistant superintendent of the Armor Packing company was sworn next, and asked:

"How long did Jesse James work at your packing house?"

"Eight years."

"What is his reputation in the community?"

"His reputation was the best. I considered him a model young man while he was in our employ."

Judge John W. Henry, of the circuit court, a former member of the supreme court, was the next witness. He said the reputation of Jesse James was good.

E. F. Swinney, cashier of the first National bank, testified next that the reputation of Jesse James was good; there was none better. Then court adjourned.

\

The Kansas City Journal reported as follows the next day's proceedings in court:

An old woman yesterday tottered into the court room where Jesse James is being tried on a charge of train robbery. Her steps were unsteady as she tremblingly felt her way over the floor to the witness stand. She was supported on the one side by a stern-faced, steely-eyed man of middle age, while on the other, guiding her with tender care, was a young woman. The hair of the old woman was whitened with the weight of years and troubles and her failing eyesight had necessitated the use of gold rimmed glasses.

That old woman was Mrs. Zerelda Samuels, the mother of Jesse James, a man who less than a quarter of a century ago was the most noted bandit of the world. Jesse has gone to join the silent majority, shot to death by a treacherous comrade. The young woman who was so solicitous for her welfare was her granddaughter, Mary James, the sister of the defendant.

As the aged woman made her way to the witness chair she was obliged to pass her grandson. He arose, pressed her hand, and was greeted with a soft smile from the grandmother's eyes.

The tension in the court room was great as Mrs. Samuels took her seat. As she sank back in the witness chair she faced the entire assemblage, and five hundred pairs of eyes were fixed upon her.

They noted the tremor of the aged hand, the glossy whiteness of the hair upon which rested a simple and becoming bonnet of black; the plain black silk dress—everything. Every ear was on the alert to hear the words which she would utter.

"Hold up your right hand and be sworn," boomed forth the clerk of the court.

Up went the right arm, but the hand was missing! Nothing but an empty sleeve—empty nearly to the elbow—greeted the vision. The minds of all, unconsciously, instantly reverted to the tragedy in which she lost that hand so many years ago, when Pinkerton detectives are said to have thrown a dynamite bomb into her house, killing an infant in her arms and maiming herself for life.

"You hereby swear that everything you say upon this stand shall be the truth, the whole truth, and nothing but the truth?"

"I do." There was nothing weak about this response.

While given in a low voice, it was clear and distinct, and after its utterance the jaws closed with the snap of determination.

"Please state to the court your name, age and residence," said Attorney Yeager, who conducted the examination.

"My name is Zerelda Samuels, I am seventy four years of age, and I live in Clay County."

"Do you know the defendant?" pointing to Jesse James.

"Yes; he is my grandson."

The examination of Mrs. Samuels elicited the fact that she had arrived at the James home the day before the train robbery, from Clay County, and that she had reached the house about noon. She said that upon her arrival Mrs. Allen Palmer, a married daughter, together with her two children, were there, but that they left that night. She testified that Jesse left with his mother, his aunt and the children, to place them on a cable car that night before 8 o'clock. She did not remember when Jesse had got back to the house, but it was some little time. It was moonlight, warm, and they were sitting upon the porch. She said that Jesse had come in the back way, around the house, and joined herself and Mary James on the porch. Some little time afterwards Mrs. James returned, and they were all seated there together when she heard the explosion. She asked Jesse what it was. She didn't remember exactly but she thought he said it was a blast at the coal mines. They went to bed about 11 o'clock.

"Was there any man there that evening to see Jesse?"

"No, sir; there was no man there at all but Jesse."

"Are you sure?"

"Yes, sir; I am."

"Why did not Jesse go to the depot with his aunt and mother."

"Because I asked him to stay with me. And I didn't think there was any use for both of them to go."

She stated most positively that Jesse did not leave his home after he had returned from the cable car that night.

Mrs. James, the mother of the defendant, was next called. She gave her age as fifty-three. She told of going to the depot with Mrs. Palmer and her children, who took the 9:05 "Katy" for Texas. She left them before the train pulled out and went straight home. When she arrived there she found Mrs. Samuels, Mary and Jesse seated upon the front porch. They remained there until about 11 o'clock and then retired. She did not hear the explosion. She is somewhat deaf. She was positive that Jesse did not leave the house after she had returned that evening.

"Call Miss Mary James," said Mr. Walsh to a deputy. The sister of the defendant came in from the witness room and took the chair. She is a sweet faced young woman of nineteen, was quietly dressed in black and wore black gloves.

"I have lived in the city for sixteen years," she said in response to a question. "I have attended the Woodland, Morse, Linwood, and Central High school."

"You are a graduate of the last?"

"Yes, sir."

She corroborated the evidence of her mother and grandmother. She said that her mother returned from the depot on the night of the robbery between 9:30 and 10 o 'clock. They were seated on the porch when she came and Jesse had not been home long.

"We heard the explosion shortly afterward," she said, "and grandma asked Jesse what it was. No, I don't remember what he answered."

"Did any man come up and ask where Jesse was that night?"

"Why, no," surprisedly.

"Was there any man there at all that night?"

"None other than Jesse."

Following is the newspaper account of my testimony given in my own behalf:

On his direct examination Jesse said he was twenty-three years old last August and had lived in Kansas City sixteen years. He went to the Morse, Linwood, Webster and High school. He went to work at the Bee Hive when he was eleven years old. Then he worked for Crittenden & Phister as an office boy for ten months. He next worked three months for the Germania Life Insurance company. He went to work at Armor's packing house June 12, 1891, and quit there January 15, 1898, and opened a cigar stand in the court house.

"Are you acquainted with W. W. Lowe?" he was asked.

"Yes, sir."

"How long had you known him prior to this robbery?"

"Since last May. I met him first in Krueger's court and he came to the court house a few times and bought cigars."

"Do you know Andy Ryan?"

"Yes; he came three or four times ta the court house to buy cigars."

"Did you ever ask Lowe how to rob a train?"

"I did not."

"Did you ever plan to rob a train?"

"I did not."

Jesse said that the night of the robbery he was shaved at 7 o'clock, at 7:30 he went home, at 8 or 8:15 he went with his mother, aunt and two cousins to the cable car. He was around Thirty-third street and Troost avenue till 9 o'clock or a little after, when he went home and stayed all night.

Jesse denied that he was at Andy Ryan's house with Lowe September 21; he denied that he wrote the card which one of the robbers gaze to the express messenger. He said he was not the man who rode in on a freight train with S. M. Downer, Sunday, August 28.

"You say you never met Lowe at any other place than you have mentioned; in Krueger's court and at your cigar stand, four or five times?" asked Prosecutor Reed.

"I never did."

"You never had any business with him?"

"Never, except to sell him cigars and tobacco, the same as any one else."

"You never had any other meeting or business or transaction with him at any time or place?"

"I never did."

"Look at the outside of this envelope and see whether or not it is your handwriting."

Reed handed Jesse the envelope of the Lowe letter.

"It looks very much like my writing, but it is not mine," answered Jesse, pronouncing each word distinctly and with emphasis.

"Look at this letter and say if you wrote it."

Jesse looked over the Lowe letter and answered as before:

"It looks very much like mine, but it is not mine."

"Didn't you take that letter to the Santa Fe yards where Lowe worked as a switchman, and didn't you leave it there for him?" asked the prosecutor.

"I did not"

"Did you go to Leeds with Lowe, Sunday, August 28?"

"I did not."

"Were you ever at Leeds?"

"Yes; about two hundred times."

"What was your business there?"

"To get the school for my sister to teach, and bicycle riding."

Jesse said that last summer he tried to induce the school directors of Leeds to give his sister Mary a place, and he rode out there a great many times on his bicycle. He was out there Sunday, August 21, on his bicycle and was in Hutchison's store.

I have given here a summary of the evidence for and against me. The arguments of the counsel to the jury consumed a whole day. The speeches were very eloquent. I have no space here to produce any part of them. The jury retired and took only one ballot, which was unanimous for my acquittal.

After my acquittal the newspapers of the West commented on it liberally. I give here a few of these editorial comments:

"Jesse James may be guilty, but we believe the weight of the evidence was in his favor."—Lexington (Mo.) Intelligencer.

"The acquittal of Jesse James will be heralded with pleasure by all who know his peculiar history. A set of scoundrels were trying to rivet a chain around him and we are glad of their failure."—Pierce City (Mo.) Democrat.

"Jesse James has been acquitted at Kansas City of the charge of train robbery. But no train robber need take any encouragement from that. The people of this state are dead set against this crime. The evidence did not show James guilty. Under the evidence as presented he ought to have been acquitted. No juror who regarded and valued his oath could have voted otherwise. The detectives made the case against Jesse James. They originated it, worked it up, found the witnesses, wrote out their confessions for them, furnished them money for their testimony, had him indicted and had charge of the prosecution, and they were employed to do this by the railroads. The detectives wanted big game. They wanted to make a big show, a spectacular demonstration. The conviction of Jesse James would terrorize train robbers more than would the conviction of twenty ordinary train robbers. So all hands joined in to send him to the penitentiary—Brunswick (Mo.) Brunswicker.

CHAPTER XII.IN CONCLUSION

In bringing this book to a close, I wish to thank, from the bottom of my heart, those friends who came to my help and support when indeed I needed friends. I know that without the moral and material support those friends gave me the conspiracy of detectives to ruin me might have been successful. I can name here only a few of those friends. Among them were Thomas T. Crittenden, who was governor of Missouri when my father was killed. Mr. Crittenden has taken a deep interest in my welfare since my boyhood, and when I was arrested for robbing a train he was one who came to my support and declared openly that he believed I was innocent. Another friend who stood by the through thick and thin was Tom Crittenden, son of the former governor. When I was a Chittenden came to me and said:

"Jesse, I have knows you since you walk a little had. I have helped you and watched yon closely, and have been very solicitous as to your fully. Tea gained my confidence and I believed in you. I want to know now if you helped to rob this train or if you knew anything about it. I want you to tell the whole truth."

I replied to him :

"Tom you are as good a friend as I have on earth. No one ever knew a James to go back on a friend. If I'd lie to you now I ought to be hung like a damned cur. I tell you I am absolutely innocent, and all I ask is a fair trial and I'll prove it."

He said to me then: "I'm going to accept your statement of your innocence as true. I believe you are telling the truth, and I 'm going to stand by you."

At that time Crittenden was a candidate for reelection to the office of County Clerk. The Kansas City "World, in commenting on this recently, said:

"The friendship existing between Tom Crittenden, county clerk, and Jesse James, jr., is quite well known in Kansas City. The newspapers referred to it often during the recent trial of the boy, on a charge of train robbery, and many marveled at evidences of fellowship so staunch as to outlive the effects of evil report against this scion of Jesse James, sr., the bandit. Mr. Crittenden never doubted the innocence of his protégé. Though the trial occurred in the heat of a political campaign, in which Mr. Crittenden was a candidate for re-election and when to avow sympathy for an accused train robber was to make enemies, still he stood by young James, and helped him with his time, money and influence.

"A political campaign was on. Crittenden was a candidate on the democratic ticket for re-election to the office of county clerk. The campaign was a warm one and the question of train robbery was an issue in it.

"Under those circumstances and in the face of that sort of campaign, it was perilous for a democratic candidate to openly avow his championship of one of the alleged train robbers. But Crittenden made no half way business of it.

"He furnished the bond for Jesse's release. He retained lawyers to defend him, and helped gather evidence to acquit him. He was criticized severely for this, and it was even said that his action would cause the defeat of all the democratic candidates. Then came the acquittal of Jesse, but not before the day of election which brought the re-election of Crittenden.

"After the acquittal, Crittenden assisted Jesse in renting and stocking a cigar store on one of the principal streets, and the young man attends strictly to business and is making money. His best friend is yet T. T. Crittenden, jr."

Other friends who came to my help were Frank P. Walsh, E. F. Swinney, R. L. Yeager, Finis C. Farr, Milton J. Oldham and Judge John W. Henry. I wish to speak also of the fair rulings made by Judge Dorsey W. Shackleford, who presided at my trial, and by his justness secured for me a fair and impartial trial.

To all of these friends I have this to say, that through no fault of mine shall they ever have cause to regret that they gave me the hand of friendship when enemies had conspired to ruin me. My conduct in the future shall be as it has been in the past. My chief aim has always been, and shall continue to be, to show by my daily life, and by strict attention to the business I have established, that I am worthy of the respect of all good citizens and of the friendship of those who choose to be my friends, and the friends of the family of Jesse James, my father.

I have one thing more to say in conclusion. I bear no ill will or feelings of malice toward anyone. Some of my best friends are men who were Federal soldiers and who fought my father and were fought by him in honorable warfare. I am sure if my father were living today he would be the friend of these old enemies and they would be friends of him. I recall that in Lexington, at the close of the war, he and the man who shot and almost killed him became afterward warm personal friends.

I have had an uphill fight. I ask the public to give me the credit of having worthy motives, and of being desirous of succeeding in the world as a business man and a good citizen of the good old State of Missouri, on whose soil my father fought and bled and suffered as few men fought and as few men suffered for.

"THE LOST CAUSE"

39206861R00065

Made in the USA
Middletown, DE
11 January 2017